NELLIE BLY

and Investigative Journalism for Kids

© 2015 by Ellen Mahoney

All rights reserved

First edition

Published by Chicago Review Press, Incorporated

814 North Franklin Street

Chicago, Illinois 60610

ISBN 978-1-61374-997-5

Library of Congress Cataloging-in-Publication Data

Mahoney, Ellen Voelckers.

  Nellie Bly and investigative journalism for kids : mighty muckrakers from the golden age to today, with 21 activities / Ellen Mahoney. — First edition.

       pages cm

  Includes bibliographical references and index.

  ISBN 978-1-61374-997-5 (trade paper)

  1. Investigative reporting—Juvenile literature.

  2. Journalism—Authorship—Juvenile literature. I. Title.

  PN4781.M24 2015

  070.4′3—dc23

2014037538

Cover and interior design: Monica Baziuk

Interior illustrations: Jim Spence

Front cover images (clockwise from left): Nellie Bly, The University of Iowa Libraries, Iowa City, Iowa; Newsboys, Library of Congress LC-DIG-nclc-03364; Ida B. Wells, Special Collections Research Center, University of Chicago Library; Bob Woodward and Carl Bernstein, *Washington Post*/Getty Images; Amy Goodman, Courtesy Democracy Now!; Upton Sinclair, Library of Congress LC-DIG-ggbain-06185

Back cover images (clockwise from left): Ida Tarbell, The Ida M. Tarbell Collection, Pelletier Library, Allegheny College; Jacob Riis, Library of Congress, LC-USZ62-47078; Annie Leonard, Lindsay France, Cornell University; *New York Times* newsroom, Library of Congress LC-DIG-ds-02106; bellows camera, courtesy Rob Niederman

Printed in the United States

5 4 3 2 1

NELLIE BLY

and Investigative Journalism for Kids

MIGHTY MUCKRAKERS
FROM THE GOLDEN AGE TO TODAY

WITH 21 ACTIVITIES

Ellen Mahoney

CHICAGO
REVIEW
PRESS

CONTENTS

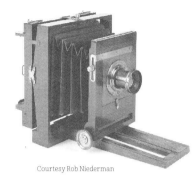
Courtesy Rob Niederman

FOREWORD

In the early 1990s, when my daughter was in middle school, I set out at her suggestion to write a detailed biography of the life of Nellie Bly. This was no easy task in those days. The newspapers that made her famous had been out of business for many years. There was no Internet to ease finding records of her work. Nellie Bly left no personal archive of papers or letters, and she had no children to preserve her legacy. Even the four books she published during the 1880s and 1890s were long out of circulation. They could only be found at a few big city libraries.

Today, two decades after my book was published, I'm happy that it remains a go-to source for learning about Nellie Bly and her place in both women's and journalism history.

The experience of getting involved with Nellie Bly continues to be gratifying. I've learned how many middle school–aged children and present-day reporters and authors still find her story inspiring—just as I did as a schoolgirl and as my own daughter did a generation later. I see it in the enthusiasm of those who compete for National History Day honors year after year, or even the graduate students I encounter who base their master's projects or dissertations on her life and impact. I see it in the numerous books about her that have been published in the last two decades and in the revival of her best newspaper stories on the Web. I see it in the documentary about her life that is still widely available and in the plays and musicals and one-woman shows that continue to be produced about her.

Nellie Bly's image appears on a commemorative US postage stamp; there are Nellie Bly artifacts on display at the Newseum in Washington, DC, and she at last has her rightful place in the National Women's Hall of Fame.

Now, 150 years after Bly's birth, comes this wonderful, historically grounded account of Nellie Bly's life and the muckrakers of her era. It includes an exciting array of activities and insight into why we continue to find this woman so remarkable a century and a half after her birth.

"Energy rightly applied and directed will accomplish anything." That is a Nellie Bly maxim, one of the many she not only said, but made it her business to live. Here's to Nellie Bly and to Ellen Mahoney for bringing her to you anew.

—Brooke Kroeger, author of *Nellie Bly: Daredevil, Reporter, Feminist*

✳

Author's collection

TIME LINE

1864 Elizabeth Jane Cochran, later known as Nellie Bly, is born in Cochran's Mills, Pennsylvania, on May 5

1865 The Civil War, which started in 1861, ends

1870 Elizabeth's father dies unexpectedly

1879 Elizabeth attends Indiana State Normal School in Indiana, Pennsylvania

1880 Elizabeth's family moves to Pittsburgh, Pennsylvania

1885 Elizabeth is hired by the *Pittsburgh Dispatch* and begins using her pen name, Nellie Bly

1886 Nellie travels to Mexico for six months as a *Pittsburgh Dispatch* foreign correspondent to investigate and write about the country

1887 Nellie relocates to New York City and is hired as a reporter by Joseph Pulitzer's *New York World*. Her first assignment is to go undercover at the Women's Lunatic Asylum on Blackwell's Island in New York

Nellie publishes *Ten Days in a Mad-House* as a series of articles in the *New York World*

Nellie publishes her first book, *Ten Days in a Mad-House*

1888 Nellie Bly publishes her second book, *Six Months in Mexico*

1889   Nellie publishes her third book, *The Mystery of Central Park*, which is a novel

Nellie sets out to travel around the world in 75 days to beat the record of Jules Verne's Phileas Fogg character in the novel *Around the World in Eighty Days*

1890   Now a celebrity, Nellie returns from her trip in 72 days

Nellie publishes her fourth book, *Nellie Bly's Book: Around the World in Seventy-Two Days*

Jacob Riis publishes his book *How the Other Half Lives: Studies Among the Tenements of New York*

1892   Ida B. Wells publishes her pamphlet, *Southern Horrors: Lynch Law in All Its Phases*

1894   Nellie writes about the Pullman strike in Chicago for the *New York World*

1895   Nellie is offered a job with the *Chicago Times-Herald* but quits within five weeks

Nellie marries businessman Robert Livingston Seaman

1904   Ida Tarbell publishes her book *The History of the Standard Oil Company*

Robert Seaman dies; Nellie becomes owner of Seaman's Iron Clad Manufacturing Company

1906   Upton Sinclair publishes his novel *The Jungle*

Teddy Roosevelt first uses the term *muck-rake* in a 1906 dedication speech in Washington, DC

1913   Nellie reports on the Woman Suffrage Procession in Washington, DC

1914   Nellie travels to Europe

World War I begins

Nellie reports on World War I from the trenches as a war correspondent for William Randolph Hearst's newspaper, the *New York Evening Journal*

1918   World War I ends

1919   Nellie returns to the United States and continues to write for the *Journal*

1922   At 57 years old, Nellie Bly dies in New York City on January 27

❋

INTRODUCTION

*

The Remarkable Nellie Bly

*

Her real name was Elizabeth Jane Cochran, but by the time she was 25 years old, Elizabeth was known all over the world as brave Nellie Bly. She was bold, daring, hardworking, and savvy—and at one point considered the best newspaper reporter in America.

Nellie Bly was a pioneer in the world of journalism. She gained an unforgettable reputation for her investigative stunt reporting that led the way for other writers to become progressive, world-changing journalists.

Nellie wasn't afraid to take big risks to cover important stories. While working for Joseph Pulitzer's *New York World* newspaper, Nellie went undercover as a mentally ill patient so she could discover firsthand what was really going on at the Women's Lunatic Asylum on Blackwell's Island. Suddenly,

Nellie Bly.

Nellie was immersed in a stark world she described as unbearably cold, unsanitary, and staffed by a number of cruel individuals who mistreated patients. Natural worries flooded her mind. *Would she be trapped there for life? Would someone arrive to get her out? What would become of all the other women?*

Her investigative reporting didn't stop there. Nellie wrote many articles by pretending to be someone else and intentionally putting herself in harm's way. She posed as a single mother with an unwanted child to uncover baby trafficking, she got herself thrown into jail to report on its deplorable conditions, and she worked in a sweatshop to witness the mistreatment of employees.

Nellie often went above and beyond her comfort zone. With only a small suitcase in hand and her confidence in tow, she traveled around the world to beat the record of the fictitious Phileas Fogg from the classic Jules Verne novel *Around the World in Eighty Days* and write about it. Soon the whole world knew about the "crazy," bold, but highly interesting Nellie Bly.

As a reporter at major newspapers such as the *Pittsburgh Dispatch*, the *New York World*, the *Chicago Times-Herald*, and the *New York Evening Journal*, Nellie wrote many articles about the ills of America and the underdog struggling to survive in an unjust world.

But she wasn't a polished journalist. Her pieces were often opinionated, self-centered, and at times one-sided. She didn't have the help of an audio recorder for interviews, so the direct quotes in her stories were from the notes she took or from her memory. She also had an uncanny and somewhat curious knack for finding jobs, quitting jobs, and then finding jobs again.

But to Nellie's credit, the plucky reporter paved the way for the forward-thinking

Nellie Bly's signature.

journalists called muckrakers, such as Jacob Riis, Ida Tarbell, Ida B. Wells, and Upton Sinclair, who you'll read about in this book. Writing for newspapers, magazines, and books, these muckrakers crusaded against disease-infested tenement houses, corporate monopolies, lynchings, and abusive labor conditions. Their investigative reporting shed light on some of society's biggest problems of the late 1800s and early 1900s caused by rapid industrialization, immigration, and urbanization. Their work was demanding and even dangerous as they tackled tough issues of crime, corruption, and civil rights. Like Nellie Bly, the muckrakers led fascinating lives, helped inform the public, and worked hard to change and improve our world.

BORN TO WRITE

"Dare to live the life you have dreamed for yourself.
Go forward and make your dreams come true."
—RALPH WALDO EMERSON

Although Nellie Bly was one of a kind, she was known by six different names throughout her lifetime. Her birth name was Elizabeth Jane Cochran, her nickname was Pink, her revised name was Elizabeth J. Cochrane, her pen name was Nellie Bly, her undercover name was Nellie Brown, and her married name was Elizabeth Cochrane Seaman. These six distinct names helped carve out her identity during her busy, tumultuous and adventurous life.

Elizabeth Jane Cochran was born on May 5, 1864, in the quaint farming town of Cochran's Mills in the southwest region of Pennsylvania. Although the Civil War (1861–1865) raged on and the bloody Battle of the Wilderness had erupted in Virginia on Elizabeth's birthday, "all was calm" in Cochran's Mills.

Elizabeth's father, Michael Cochran, and her mother, Mary Jane Cochran, were married in 1858. It was a second marriage for both Michael and Mary Jane, whose first spouses had died. Michael already had 10 children from his previous marriage when he married Mary Jane, and their first daughter together, Elizabeth Jane Cochran, aka Nellie Bly, became the 13th of 15 children in the large combined Cochran clan. In addition to five stepsisters and five stepbrothers, Elizabeth had two older brothers named Albert and Charles, a younger sister named Catherine May, and a younger brother named Harry.

Nellie Bly's home in Cochran's Mills, Pennsylvania.

Carnegie Library of Pittsburgh

Michael's father, Robert Cochran, was born in County Derry, Ireland, in the late 1700s. He emigrated from Ireland as a young man and moved to Baltimore, Maryland, where he met and married Catherine Risher. Robert and Catherine Cochran then settled in southwestern Pennsylvania in the early 1800s.

Michael Cochran was born in 1810 and grew up in the small coal-mining town of Apollo in Armstrong County, Pennsylvania. Apollo is located on the Kiskiminetas River, not far from what would later become Cochran's Mills. Robert Cochran died before Michael was five years old, and his mother, Catherine, played a key role in his upbringing, encouraging him to work hard and learn a trade.

During his early career Michael was an accomplished blacksmith and cutler, and he later became involved in local and state politics. A respected and prominent individual in Apollo, he was elected justice of the peace in 1840 when he was 30 years old.

In 1845, about 19 years before Elizabeth was born, Michael began to invest in real estate. He bought land and property in a hamlet of Armstrong County called Pitts' Mills that was located a few miles from Apollo and about 45 miles from Pittsburgh.

The landmark in Pitts' Mills was a large gristmill with a waterwheel situated on the town's winding waterway called Crooked Creek.

Powered by the rushing currents of the creek, the waterwheel provided ample energy to grind a variety of locally grown grains into flour and livestock feed. Farmers would haul their wheat, corn, buckwheat, oats, and rye to the gristmill and would later sell the flour and feed to the surrounding communities.

Michael continued to invest in and improve Pitts' Mills, making smart business choices along the way. He opened a grocery store in town, which provided the small community with much-needed items such as food products and dry goods as well as shoes, boots, hats, caps, and notions (thread, needles, buttons). In time, Michael earned a reputation as a highly regarded, self-made businessman.

In 1850, at 40 years old, Michael was elected to be associate justice for Armstrong County. From then on, the townsfolk respectfully called him Judge. Five years later in 1855, the Pitts' Mills name was changed to Cochran's Mills, in honor of Elizabeth's father.

Cochran's Mills was a picturesque place to grow up. White clapboard farmhouses, dirt roads, covered bridges, horse-drawn carriages, and women wearing long skirts and carrying parasols were common sights. Ash, elm, and hemlock trees and a wide variety of herbs and flowers grew along the banks of Crooked Creek, which was home to many fish including smallmouth bass, pumpkinseed sunfish, and catfish.

Nellie's mother, Mary Jane Cochran.
Linda Henry Champanier

Nellie's father, Judge Michael Cochran.
Linda Henry Champanier

The town of Cochran's Mills continued to flourish and eventually offered its residents a "doctor, a dentist, a school and a post office, as well as several small businesses."

PINK

DURING THE years following the Civil War when Elizabeth was learning to walk, talk, run, and read, children wore clothing that was very different from today's outfits. Clothing was typically handmade or sewn on hand-cranked or foot-powered treadle sewing machines. Boys wore cotton or flannel shirts, jackets, bib overalls, and trousers or knee breeches (knickers) held up with suspenders. Toddlers and younger boys sometimes wore simple dresses.

Girls wore shirtwaist dresses that were either full-length or mid-calf. The dresses had fitted bodices, gathered sleeves, and flouncy skirts with petticoats or small hoops to make them wide and full. Bloomers and camisoles were used as undergarments, and pinafores were worn over dresses or skirts like aprons.

Clothes were often sewn using drab and muted fabric colors such as dark gray, black, brown, dark blue, or green. But Elizabeth's mother wanted a different, more colorful shade for her first-born daughter's clothes. Pink! It wasn't long before family members and friends were calling Elizabeth Jane Cochran "Pink" or "Pinkey," on behalf of this flashy, fun color.

The young Cochran girl with the unusual nickname was a bright sight to see. The vibrant, rosy color of her clothes made her stand out in a crowd, and she learned early on that getting attention could have positive results. Life seemed good, and grand adventures were on the horizon.

In 1869 when Pink was five, her father moved the family to his hometown of Apollo to live in an attractive and spacious two-and-a-half-story home he built for them. The home stood on a large lot that had plenty of room for Pink, her sister, her brothers, and their two dogs to run and play. And, there was ample pasture for the family cow that provided milk and the family horse that pulled their carriage.

Apollo had grown since Michael was a child and was now home to nearly 760 people. Young Pink seemed to have an idyllic life—loving parents, a large family to enjoy, a stately new home

Children's clothing when Nellie Bly was young.
Courtesy Karen's Whimsy

WORDS SUCH AS *FEISTY* and *daredevil* are often used to describe Nellie Bly. For this activity, draw your name in large bubble letters and write words inside each letter that describe who you are.

You'll Need

* Printer paper, 8½ by 11-inches (21.6 by 28 cm)
* Scissors
* Ruler
* Pencil
* Marker
* Eraser
* Construction paper
* Craft glue or glue stick
* Colored pencils

1. Fold a piece of printer paper in half and cut on the folded line. Use a half sheet of paper (placed vertically) for each letter of your name.

2. With a ruler and pencil, draw two lines horizontally across the page, 3 inches (7.6 cm) apart and centered in the approximate middle of the page. Now, using these

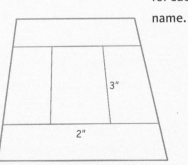

two lines, draw a 2-inch-wide-by-3-inch-tall (5.1-cm-wide-by-7.6-cm-tall) rectangle.

3. Print the first letter of your name, using the entire rectangle.

4. Draw oval shapes around the lines of the letter until the letter looks inflated, like a bubble. Outline the letter with a marker and erase all pencil lines.

5. Cut out the letter.

6. Repeat steps one through five for each letter of your name.

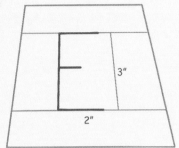

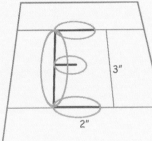

7. Arrange your bubble letters on a piece of construction paper; it's OK if letters overlap.

8. Glue down the letters.

9. Inside each letter, write words that describe who you are.

10. Use colored pencils to decorate each letter.

Nellie's home in Apollo, Pennsylvania. Apollo Area Historical Society

with a big yard, a picture-perfect hometown, and even a new baby brother named Harry.

FROM PINK TO BLUE

BUT IN 1870, when Pink was six years old, everything turned upside down. Suddenly and very unexpectedly, Pink's beloved father died, which threw the family into a terrible tailspin and altered their lives forever.

When Judge Cochran died, Mary Jane learned he had not written a will for his large family. This meant there were no specifications on how his estate should be divided among all the heirs and where the Cochran family money should go. After about two months, the Armstrong County court intervened to sort out the inheritance, and Judge Cochran's property (including his land in Cochran's Mills and the brand-new home in Apollo), was auctioned off.

Dividing the estate was complicated. Under Pennsylvania law, Mary Jane was entitled to receive about one-third of the money from Judge Cochran's estate for the rest of her life. All of Mary Jane's children were to receive equal amounts of money from the remaining two-thirds of the estate. The town banker, Colonel Samuel Jackson, was appointed to watch over and distribute the children's trust funds, and the younger children would receive their funds when they were older.

Now, because their home had been auctioned off, Mary Jane needed to find a new place to live with Albert, Charles, Pink, Catherine, and baby Harry. Judge Cochran's older children from his first marriage now lived in their own homes, and his youngest son, William Worth Cochran, had died during the Civil War.

Mary Jane moved the family to a much smaller house a few streets over from the Apollo home. She was able to bring along their furniture and household items as well as the cow, the horse, and one of their dogs. It was a difficult time for Mary Jane, who was dealing with the sorrow of losing her husband, the grief her children felt missing their father, and the utter disruption in their lives. But life went on.

The Cochran children walked to school with neighborhood friends, and there were fun things to do in Apollo like sledding and skating in winter, and playing hide-and-seek and fishing in summer. Mary Jane made sure there was enough money for Pink to learn to play the piano and organ and take horseback riding lessons, which she loved to do.

In 1873 when Pink was nine years old, her mother married again. Mary Jane exchanged vows with John Jackson Ford, a Civil War veteran and widower, who preferred to be called Jack. Jack's wife had died six months earlier, and he had no children from his previous marriage. But he did come into this new marriage with debt and an angry temperament. He turned out to be "a mean and abusive drunk."

Over the next few years, as Pink entered the important years of adolescence, her life was a constant nightmare caused by Jack's drunken rages, his abusive and threatening behavior toward her mother, and his fights with her brother Albert.

In 1878, when Pink was 14, Mary Jane filed for divorce in Armstrong County Court. This took a lot of courage because divorce was not common or accepted at this time. Yet, many neighbors and friends, as well as Pink and Albert, went to court to provide crucial testimony on behalf of their mother's case and to convince the judge that John Jackson Ford was cruel and dangerous.

Pink's testimony was poignant. Referring to her stepfather as "Ford," she defended her mother with conviction: "My age is 14 years. I live with my mother. I was present when mother was married to J. J. Ford. I [had] seen them married about six years ago. Ford has been generally drunk since they were married. When drunk, he is very cross and cross when sober."

Pink went on. "[I have] seen mother vexed on account of his swearing and bad names and [I've] seen her cry. Ford threatened to do mother harm. Mother was afraid of him."

In 1879 the court granted Mary Jane a divorce. By now, John Jackson Ford had left town and was long gone. Mary Jane immediately dropped the last name Ford and starting using her Cochran surname once again.

Pink was understandably shaken and discouraged by the previous eight years of her life. Losing her father and her affluent lifestyle was heart-wrenching and difficult, but having to live with an abusive stepfather was devastating. In only a few short years Pink had experienced so much as a child. She learned that life could change from pleasant to painful in the blink of an eye, that loved ones could die and leave her, that there could be plenty of money or not enough, and that she could have a father she adored or a father figure she dreaded. But most important, she learned the importance of self-reliance. Pink wanted something better for her life, and she was determined to get it.

THE NEW NORMAL

WATCHING HER mother struggle with finances and scrape by, Pink realized it would be a smart idea to get a job so she would be able to fend for

herself. Going off to school and getting an education could be her ticket to success.

Pink heard about a new state-of-the-art school called the Indiana State Normal School located in Indiana, Pennsylvania, which was only 15 miles from her home in Apollo. The Normal School offered two- to three-year programs to train students in teaching or business. Pink decided to enroll in the school and become a teacher. To figure out how to pay for tuition, Pink met with her court-appointed guardian, Colonel Samuel Jackson. Jackson assured Pink she would have enough money to graduate in three years.

Feeling empowered and excited about this new direction in her life, 15-year-old Pink enrolled in the school for the fall semester of 1879. While filling out enrollment forms, she dropped her nickname and came up with the more sophisticated moniker of Elizabeth J. Cochrane, curiously adding an *e* to the end of her last name. Over time, Mary Jane and Elizabeth's siblings also began to spell their last name as *Cochrane*.

Elizabeth enjoyed staying in the John Sutton Hall dormitory at the Indiana State Normal School and attending classes in everything from writing to math to art. She was happy and filled with hope.

Samuel Jackson paid Elizabeth's expenses as promised, but it soon became apparent her money was running out. When Elizabeth returned to Apollo for a semester break, she was alarmed to

Indiana State Normal School in Indiana, Pennsylvania.

Special Collections & University Archives, Indiana University of Pennsylvania

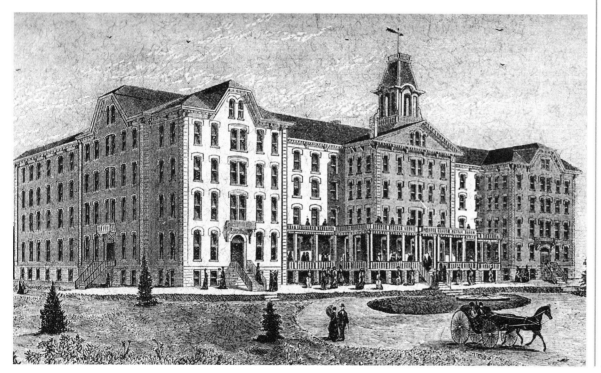

find out there wasn't enough money for her to return to school the following spring semester. And no one, including Jackson, reached out to help her find a way to stay in school.

Elizabeth was angry and disappointed at Jackson for his perceived mismanagement of the money he promised would be there for her. She felt she had been treated unfairly, and by bitter surprise, Elizabeth realized her commendable attempts for a higher education had failed and her plans to become a teacher were over. She never returned to the Normal School to finish her exams.

Leaving the Indiana State Normal School after only one semester couldn't have been easy for Elizabeth. News of the event probably spread fast in her small hometown of Apollo, and Elizabeth was likely at the receiving end of many embarrassing questions. *What happened at school? What went wrong? Were your courses too hard? Why did you leave? What will you do?*

It was 1880 and Elizabeth was 16 years old. She needed a whole new plan.

ONWARD TO THE CITY OF BRIDGES

ALBERT AND Charles had already left home and were trying to make a living in Pittsburgh, Pennsylvania, a manufacturing and shipping hub located about 30 miles south of Apollo.

Early map of Pittsburgh, Pennsylvania.
Library of Congress LC-DIG-pga-03733

Often called the City of Bridges for its many bridges that crossed the town's three large Allegheny, Monongahela, and Ohio rivers, Pittsburgh was an enormous metropolis compared to Apollo and offered new jobs and employment. Also known as the City of Steel for its burgeoning steel industry, Pittsburgh was overflowing with factories that sent blackish smoke and soot into the air and onto the city.

Wanting a fresh start, Mary Jane packed up a few family belongings and moved Elizabeth,

A Penny for Your Thoughts?

NORTH AMERICA'S first newspaper looked like it had a bad case of failed spell-check. Named *Publick Occurrences Both Forreign and Domestick*, this early Boston newspaper was published on September 25, 1690, by Benjamin Harris, a progressive publisher from London who set out to report news fairly and accurately in America. The paper was only four pages long and was shut down after only one issue for its controversial content. But it was a start.

The next American newspaper, *The Boston News-Letter*, was published 14 years later in 1704. Hundreds of newly formed newspapers such as the *Boston Gazette*, the *American Weekly Mercury*, and the *New-England Courant* were published over the following years. They had limited circulation and staff, and the publisher was often the reporter and editor as well. Plus, these papers were very expensive.

Newsboy sells a "penny paper."
Library of Congress LC-DIG-nclc-03574

The 1800s brought industrial change. With advances in the high-speed, steam-powered printing press, it was possible to print many newspapers faster, more efficiently, and on larger papers. The telegraph enabled information to be sent to other cities. Newspapers focused on politics or business and were full of ads and articles without many images.

There were big changes for newspapers in the 1830s. Papers started reaching out to a broader, more diverse audience of middle- and working-class readers who wanted a paper they could afford and one that offered more human-interest stories. Along came the "penny paper." These inexpensive daily papers cost only one cent, compared to previous six-cent papers. With the lower cost, circulation soared along with literacy. Over the next 70 years, large urban papers such as the *Pittsburgh Dispatch* (where Nellie Bly got her start) became commonplace and were sold on street corners by young boys (and some girls) called newsies. Many historians agree the "golden age of newspapers" lasted from the arrival of penny papers in the 1830s until the arrival of radio in the 1930s.

Catherine, and Harry to Pittsburgh. She found a row house in a working-class neighborhood just north of Pittsburgh called Allegheny City, and Albert and Charles moved in with them. To help bring in extra money to meet costs over the following years, Mary Jane took in boarders. For the next five years, Elizabeth most likely earned money as a housekeeper, nanny, or tutor to help with household expenses.

In 1885 when Elizabeth was 21, her life changed dramatically, thanks to her city newspaper. Elizabeth had become an avid reader of the *Pittsburgh Dispatch* newspaper, and she took a particular interest in reading the highly popular columns of writer Erasmus Wilson, who penned the paper's *Quiet Observer* column. But one morning, Elizabeth became infuriated after reading one of Wilson's columns. Wilson had begun to write about women's roles in the world and expressed many opinions Elizabeth didn't like. At a time when many women were fighting for equal rights and the right to vote, Wilson wrote about how wives, mothers, and daughters should stay in the home and take pride and joy in their domestic role of cleaning and cooking. He wrote about how a woman who ventured outside her home and into the business world would be a "monstrosity" and added, "there is no greater abnormity than a woman in breeches, unless it is a man in petticoats."

Elizabeth fumed, thinking his words were sexist and wrong. She knew her own mother was miserable when she was married to John Jackson Ford, and Elizabeth had her own aspirations to work outside the home and have a career. So, she decided to take action. Elizabeth picked up a pen, a large sheet of paper, and wrote a letter to George Madden, who was editor of the *Dispatch*. Her honest, passionate letter to the editor challenged Wilson's opinions and provided real-life information to contradict the *Quiet Observer*'s conservative point of view. Elizabeth signed her letter "Lonely Orphan Girl," gave no return address, and popped the missive in the mail.

When Madden received Elizabeth's letter, he was surprised. Written on oversized paper, the letter was riddled with poor grammar, bad spelling, and confusing punctuation. But Madden could hear the voice within the words. He knew the Lonely Orphan Girl had something to say, and from what he could tell, she had natural writing talent. He felt compelled to contact the unknown writer and posted a note in the Saturday, January 17, 1885, *Dispatch* that said, "If the writer of the communication signed 'Lonely Orphan Girl' will send her name and address to this office, merely as a guarantee of good faith, she will confer a favor and receive the information she desires."

When Elizabeth read the paper on Saturday, she saw Madden's note and knew it was for her.

Elizabeth felt excited the editor had responded to her letter and probably shared the news with her mother and family. But instead of writing George Madden a letter in reply, Elizabeth decided to meet with him face-to-face.

Without delay, she went to the *Dispatch* headquarters in downtown Pittsburgh. Wearing her best floor-length overcoat and fur turban, Elizabeth climbed the stairwell of the tall newspaper building en route to the editor's office. She probably wondered if Madden and Wilson would be the gruff, hard-nosed newspapermen she imagined them to be. But she put her fears aside and went anyway. This was a smart move, because Elizabeth discovered George Madden was open and friendly, and Erasmus Wilson was a kind gentleman who would eventually become a longtime friend.

After talking with Elizabeth, Madden decided to give her a chance to write. It would be a test of sorts, to see what she could do. He asked her to write about the roles of women and to focus on women in the home. After many years of working odd jobs for little pay and no specific career on the horizon, Elizabeth must have felt overjoyed with the challenge. She went straight home and got right to work. In a few days, she sent her first article to the editor.

Madden was impressed with Elizabeth's article about hardworking, low-income women who long for decent employment. He edited her

The *Pittsburgh Dispatch* building.
Wikimedia Commons

Pittsburgh Dispatch columnist
Erasmus Wilson. Carnegie Library of Pittsburgh

did! Elizabeth pitched an idea about the controversial subject of divorce, and he gave her the go-ahead to write it.

But first, Madden knew Elizabeth needed a new pen name, a byline, for her writing; Orphan Girl wouldn't work well in the long run.

Pen names were par for the course for women journalists at the time. Another woman writer at the *Dispatch* had chosen the byline Bessie Bramble. Elizabeth needed a catchy name readers would remember. Someone at the newspaper cleverly suggested the name Nelly Bly, which was the title of a minstrel song from the popular Pittsburgh songwriter Stephen Foster. Madden loved the byline but misspelled it as "Nellie Bly" in his excitement and haste. But the byline worked and it stuck.

Nellie's second article about divorce was soon published with the eye-catching headline, MAD MARRIAGES. When Nellie suggested writing a series of articles about workshop girls employed in Pittsburgh factories, Madden hired her as a staff writer for a salary of five dollars a week. Nellie wrote eight articles for the workshop series, which were published each Sunday in the *Dispatch* over the following two months.

Everything in Elizabeth's life had changed so quickly. Suddenly she had a new identity and purpose as the cub reporter Nellie Bly. She was making money and had the beginnings of a career.

words to correct the grammar and published her piece in the January 25, 1885, Sunday edition of the *Dispatch*. The article was titled THE GIRL PUZZLE, signed by "Orphan Girl," and placed prominently above the fold where readers could easily see it.

GREETINGS, NELLIE BLY

MADDEN PAID Elizabeth for THE GIRL PUZZLE article and asked if she had any more ideas. She

But Nellie was thrust into a world of journalism that was dominated by men who were considered tougher and better skilled to go into the field and report on topics such as crime, corruption, barroom brawls, and dirty politics. Being a reporter meant heading out into the world no matter what time of day, where a story happened, or how bad the weather was. It wasn't customary in the 1880s for a woman to travel alone at night, research a story in a blinding blizzard, travel to a sketchy part of town, or report on a dangerous story such as a murder, a building fire, or a factory accident.

But Nellie was up for the challenge. Although she wasn't a polished writer or a seasoned journalist, she was able to write compelling, provocative, and descriptive pieces that readers found interesting and relevant. For inspiration, she wrote about her life, the world around her, and the difficult issues that affected her directly, such as divorce, finding a job, or the challenges of being a woman. And, like Erasmus Wilson, Nellie was also a quiet observer. She looked at her community, wondered about it, and worried about it.

At home in Allegheny City, Nellie could chat with the many different people who boarded with her family. She reached out to the boarders, asking important questions: *What is your life like? What do you do for a living? How is it going?* She listened closely and then put her ideas down

WHEN NELLIE BLY READ Erasmus Wilson's columns in the *Pittsburgh Dispatch*, she felt angry. But she didn't just fume; she did something about it.

Nellie wrote a letter to *Dispatch* editor George Madden and told him exactly what she thought about Wilson's words. This poignant letter changed Nellie's life. Impressed by her words, Madden hired Nellie as a reporter, which launched her writing career. In this activity you'll write a letter to the editor about something you feel strongly about.

You'll Need

* Current newspapers
* Pencil or pen
* Writing paper
* Envelope
* Stamp
* Computer and printer (optional)

1. Go to the *Letters to the Editor* section of a newspaper. You'll find guidelines on how to write your letter: word count, how to submit your piece (by e-mail or mail), and contact information.

2. Read examples of published *Letters to the Editor.*

3. Choose a topic to write about. Are you unhappy about something in your community? Would you like to respond to an article you read? Is there something positive you'd like to share?

4. Write your letter. Letters are usually one to three paragraphs long and fewer than about 200 words. Remember to back up your opinions with examples.

5. Reread your letter and correct any mistakes. Then sign it, provide your contact information, and submit it to the newspaper. Send your letter to only one publication at a time. Editors receive thousands of submissions and publish only a fraction of the letters that arrive on their desks. Writers are typically contacted only if their letters will be published.

6. If your letter is published, cut it out and save it as a writing sample called a "clip."

CREATE A LIFE MOTTO

A MOTTO IS A PHRASE that sums up an idea and is often inspirational. Nellie Bly's motto above gave her positive direction in her life. A motto can inspire you to move toward your future dreams. A few well-known mottos include: "Never give up," "Be true to yourself," or "Honesty is the best policy."

You'll Need
* Pencil or pen
* Writing paper

1. Think about the things that are important to you. Ideas might come from a book, the lyrics of a song, words from a poem, dialogue from a movie, or something someone has shared with you.

2. Come up with a motto using your own words. Think about thoughts you'd like to live by.

3. Write a few mottos on paper and choose your favorite one.

4. You might like to keep your motto somewhere you can easily see it, such as on the cover of your notebook or on a bulletin board in your room.

✻

"Energy rightly applied
and directed
will accomplish anything."
—Nellie Bly

✻

on paper in vivid detail for others to read. This natural "nose for news" and curiosity about people launched Elizabeth on a writing career that spanned her entire life.

Women writers in the late 1880s typically wrote about the arts, fashion, food, society, and gardening, and Madden also wanted Nellie to write about these subjects. But Nellie preferred to write more than just fashion features, and, fortunately, Madden gave her a chance to do so. Nellie wrote about a religious sect in Pennsylvania called the Harmony Society, a woman who owned an opera company, a woman who was an unusual musical prodigy, a Civil War hero from her hometown, and the environmental causes of hay fever.

Feeling inspired and confident, Nellie angled for her own column titled *Nellie Bly*, and Madden consented. Her column wasn't an immediate hit, but when Nellie wrote about women's rights issues, readers responded positively to her distinct voice. Unfortunately, Madden discontinued Nellie's column and asked her to write conservative women's pieces on topics such as butterflies, rubber raincoats, and hair care products, which she detested.

Frustrated with this type of writing, Nellie approached Madden with a new idea. She had heard boarders staying at her mother's home talk about how it was possible to take a train all the way from Pennsylvania to Mexico. This sounded incredibly exciting to Nellie, and she asked Madden if she could become a freelance foreign correspondent. She would write from out of the country, and her series would be called *Nellie in Mexico!*

Madden liked many of Nellie's ideas, but he wasn't keen on this plan that seemed dangerous, unpredictable, and far-fetched. He insisted Nellie not go.

But the daring young journalist was determined to keep writing, get paid, and make a difference in the world. She finally convinced Madden to give his consent, and she was on her way.

✳

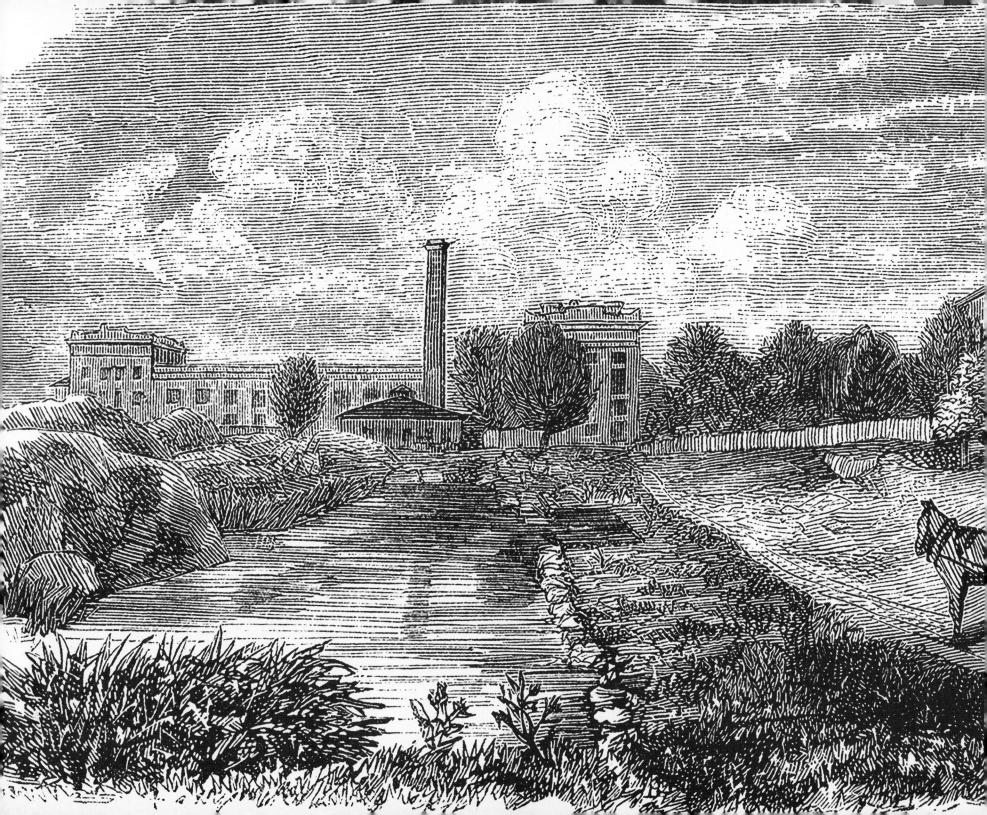

FROM MEXICO TO THE MADHOUSE

"I was too impatient to work along at the usual duties assigned women on newspapers, so I conceived the idea of going away as a correspondent."

—NELLIE BLY

Nellie was excited about the possibility of living in a foreign country, and the extensive railway systems in the United States and Mexico would enable her to get to Mexico in a matter of days. Accompanied by her mother, who acted as her chaperone, Nellie traveled over thousands of miles of railroad tracks from Pittsburgh, Pennsylvania, to the City of Mexico (Mexico City), Mexico. They planned to stay in the country for six months.

Ready to describe whatever she encountered, Nellie always had a pencil and paper in hand to document her journey. Her highly descriptive words gave readers an idea of what it was like to travel from one part of the world to another. When her train arrived in El Paso, Texas, on the border of Mexico, she wrote, "Three days after leaving Pittsburgh we awoke one morning to find ourselves in the lap of summer. For a moment it seemed a dream. When the porter had made up our bunks the evening previous, the surrounding country had been covered with a snowy blanket. When we awoke the trees were in leaf and the balmy breeze mocked our wraps."

Over the next six months Nellie dove wholeheartedly into this daring new adventure, and

Nellie was able to visit Mexico thanks to train travel.
Library of Congress LC-USZ62-48234

Nellie visited cathedrals when she was in Mexico.
Library of Congress LC-USZ62-138421

her writing blossomed. Her many handwritten articles, which were sometimes messy and difficult to read, were sent to George Madden, edited by Wilson, and published in the *Dispatch* under the series headline, NELLIE IN MEXICO, which she had proposed.

Her stories were often published by other newspapers in the United States. The articles later became the basis of Nellie's book, *Six Months in Mexico*, published by American Publishers Corporation in 1888 and dedicated to her editor, George Madden.

In Mexico, the young reporter ventured all around Mexico City and also traveled to distant towns to write about everything she discovered. Although she didn't know the Spanish language used in Mexico, Nellie found ways to meet English-speaking individuals, such as other journalists, so she could understand and write about the country's history, foods, culture, and people. Her daily itinerary was always full with frequent visits to homes, markets, post offices, libraries, cathedrals, and shrines.

Nellie also attended special events such as music festivals and romantic weddings, and she wrote extensively about terrifying bullfights. "At a fight two weeks ago one man was gored almost to death, another had his arm broken, and a woman, who had witnessed this from her seat, entered the ring and tried to kill the bull. She was caught on its horns and carried once around the ring and whirled around in her perilous position like a top . . . the bull cast the woman to the ground, devoid of clothing and badly bruised, but alive."

Nellie was naturally skilled at this type of descriptive writing. For example, she could describe a simple item such as butter with zest: "Butter is seldom seen in Mexico. The only way they have of getting it, is by its forming from the rocking on the burro's back while being brought to town. It is skimmed off the milk by the hand and is sold at a big price. It is never salted. The butter is always wrapped in corn husks, looking exactly like an ear of corn until it is opened."

On a day trip to Jalapa, she described the town with rich detail. "Jalapa has a population of 12,400, and an elevation of 4,335 feet. The climate is cool, the soil fertile, and the town never visited by contagious diseases. All around are plantations of coffee, tobacco, vanilla, cotton, maize, and jalapa—the well-known old medicine, which was a remedy for every known ill to which flesh is heir to. Jalapa is pronounced as though it were spelled with an *h*, with a soft sound to the *a*—Halapah."

Although she carefully avoided writing about controversial political issues or how the country was governed, one of her articles raised red flags. She had written about how a local newspaper journalist was arrested for criticizing the Mexican government, and when word got back

Nellie Bly at 21.
Wikimedia Commons PD-Art

PERSONALIZE A REPORTER'S NOTEBOOK

AS A REPORTER, Nellie Bly needed to be able to take notes. Even though we live in a digital world with computers, cell phones, laptops, and audio recorders, journalists still use simple reporters' notebooks to interview people and jot down information for their stories. These compact notebooks are helpful tools for reporters.

You'll Need

* Spiral reporter's notebook 4-by-8-inch (10.1-cm-by-20.3-cm)
* Construction paper
* Pencil
* Scissors
* Craft glue or glue stick
* Colorful images of people from magazines
* Computer and printer (optional)
* Ruler
* Card stock

1. Place the cover of your reporter's notebook over construction paper and trace it. Cut out what you've traced and glue the paper to the notebook cover.

2. Make an inspirational people collage on the cover. First, find a diverse collection of people's faces from recycled magazines that are about 1-inch (2.5 cm) in size. You'll need about 28 images in total. You can also find and print online images. Think about individuals you admire and people who inspire you, such as actors, athletes, authors, journalists, musicians, or politicians.

3. Use a ruler to make a 1-by-1-inch (2.5 by 2.5-cm) square pattern on card stock. Cut out this square and use it as a pattern.

4. Place the 1-inch (2.5 cm) square pattern over images of faces that are small enough to fit within the inch square and outline. Follow the outline of the square and cut out the faces.

5. Arrange the faces on your notebook cover and glue them down. It's OK to trim the squares so they'll fit.

6. To include your name on the cover, cut a ½-by-4-inch (1.3-cm-by-10.1-cm) strip of construction paper and glue it across the base of your notebook. Write your name on this strip.

7. Trim any excess paper from the edges of the cover.

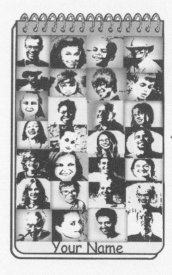

to Mexican officials, Nellie realized she was in trouble. With the prospect of winding up in a Mexican jail, she decided it was time to head home.

When Nellie returned to Pittsburgh in June 1886, she continued to write about Mexico. But now her words were as angry as they were vivid. With freedom to express herself in the United States, she wrote more about the corruption in Mexico than its beautiful countryside. Her articles criticized Mexico's leadership, its politics, and its censorship of the media. She even called Mexican President Porfirio Díaz's government "the worst monarchy in existence."

Nellie was also dealing with personal issues at this time. Still angry about having to drop out of the Indiana State Normal School when she was 15, she blamed her former guardian, banker Samuel Jackson, for this huge disappointment. Now of legal age, Nellie decided to return to her hometown of Apollo and confront the banker in court. She charged him with mismanagement of the modest inheritance she rightly deserved after her father's death. During the legal proceedings it was discovered that Jackson kept sloppy financial records and had misled Nellie into believing there was adequate funding for her to graduate from school and become a teacher one day. The case dragged on and was eventually dropped. But Nellie had learned a lifelong lesson about standing up for herself.

The Newsies' Life

IN THE 1800s in America, young boys got their start in the newspaper industry at 8, 9, or 10 years of age. They'd get up at the crack of dawn and throw on a shirt, knickers, suspenders, and a cap. After grabbing a bundle of papers hot off the press, they'd stand on busy street corners waving and hollering, "Extra! Extra! Read all about it!" with the high hopes of earning some cash for food or rent.

Called "newsies," these young newspaper boys (and sometimes girls) were often orphans or immigrant children who desperately wanted to make money. They sold daily newspapers in large cities such as New York, Boston, Philadelphia, or Chicago. As the circulation of newspapers grew, so did the ranks of newsies who missed school and braved stormy weather and big-city childhood diseases like typhoid to make a buck.

It was a rough way to make money, and it wasn't fair. Newsies bought their papers every day with cash out of their own pockets. If they didn't sell most of their papers, they lost money. In July 1899, sick of hard work and lost wages, the New York City newsies went on strike. The strike lasted just a week, and the outcome was positive. Fearing the loss of their needed newsies, the newspaper publishers agreed to buy back any papers the boys hadn't sold.

The highly visible newsies brought attention to the problem of child labor in big cities, and the US government eventually passed laws to protect child workers. The Fair Labor Standards Act was passed in 1938 and set federal regulations for child labor.

Newsboys at work. Library of Congress LC-DIG-nclc-03364

Nellie soon realized she needed to make more money to earn a living than freelance work could provide. Fortunately, Madden hired her full time at the *Dispatch* again, upped her salary, and gave her a new reporting beat to cover arts and culture in Pittsburgh. It seemed like a great fit because Nellie had done such an eloquent job describing the Mexican lifestyle with flourish and detail. For a while, she was happy to have a job at the *Dispatch* again.

But after a few months she became bored. The young journalist had gained gutsy real-life experience and confidence as a foreign correspondent in Mexico. She had slept in uncomfortable beds, ate foods she detested, met all sorts of strangers, and found ways to communicate in a foreign language. She wasn't afraid to watch gory bullfights, visit graveyards, or learn about Mexican jails. Writing artsy stories for the women's page just wasn't going to cut it.

One day she simply didn't show up for work. The only clue to her whereabouts was a note she left on Erasmus Wilson's desk that simply said, "I am off to New York. Look out for me."

NEW YORK CITY BY STORM

WHEN NELLIE set out for New York City in the spring of 1887, she knew it was a vibrant hub for newspaper reporters, and she wanted in. Major daily newspapers such as the *New York World* (the *World*), the *Sun*, the *Herald*, the *Tribune*, and the *Times* were all headquartered in an area of the city called Park Row that was nicknamed "Newspaper Row." It was the place to be for a journalist. Nellie quickly found a one-bedroom apartment and started looking for work.

Armed with a portfolio chock-full of clips she'd written for the *Dispatch*, Nellie couldn't wait to see her byline in the *World*, the paper she wanted to work at most of all. The *World* was owned by successful newspaperman Joseph Pulitzer, whose name honors Pulitzer Prize–winning writers today.

For months Nellie pounded the pavement in search of employment. But, to her surprise and frustration, she couldn't get past the gatekeepers who stood like armed guards at the doorways of the large Park Row newspaper buildings.

When Nellie's money ran out, she started freelancing for the *Dispatch* again, writing feature stories about tried-and-true subjects such as women's fashion and footwear. Fortunately, her life was about to change again. In an unusual and roundabout way, her freelance work with the *Dispatch* finally helped Nellie get her foot in the door in New York. It all started with a young woman who sent Nellie a letter at the *Dispatch*, asking about the challenges of becoming a reporter in New York City. This gave Nellie the great idea to write an article about this very

"I keep six honest serving-men
(They taught me all I knew);
Their names are What and Why and When
And How and Where and Who."
　—Rudyard Kipling, *The Elephant's Child*

WHEN REPORTERS are hot on the trail of a story, they need to be able to get information quickly, accurately, and completely. One technique used by many journalists is called the 5Ws, from the words: *who*, *what*, *when*, *where*, and *why*.

✳ Who is the story about?

✳ What happened?

✳ When did the story take place?

✳ Where did the story take place?

✳ Why is the story important?

You'll Need

✳ Small bowl

✳ Printer paper 8½ by 11-inches (21.6 by 28 cm)

✳ Marker

✳ Ruler

✳ Newspaper article

✳ Scissors

✳ Craft glue or glue stick

1. Place the bowl on the paper. Using a marker, trace around the bowl to draw a circle.

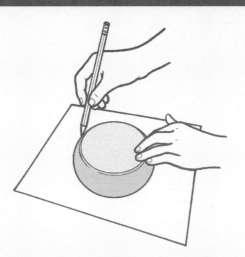

2. Use a ruler or straightedge to draw a line dividing the circle in half horizontally. Next, divide the lower half into two sections and the upper half into three sections, as shown, to create a pie chart.

3. In the lower two sections of your pie chart, write the words, *What* and *Why*. In the upper three sections write the words, *Who*, *When*, and *Where*.

4. Look through a newspaper and find an article that interests you and is OK to cut out. It might be a sports story, a food story, or a science story.

5. Read the article and hunt for the 5Ws. Circle *who* the article is about. Circle *what* happened. Circle *when* the story happened. Circle *where* the story took place. And circle *why* you think the story is important.

6. Cut out the areas of the article you've circled and paste them into the appropriate sections of your chart. You'll now have an idea of the whole story in terms of the 5Ws.

"Newspaper Row," New York City.

Her article about the struggles of women reporters trying to find work at New York City newspapers was first published in the *Dispatch* and then printed in other papers. It was a great showcase of Nellie's work as a journalist.

Unfortunately, she still could not find work in the male-dominated newspaper world. On top of it all, Nellie had rotten luck; she lost her purse with all of her savings. That day, Nellie returned to her one-room apartment feeling discouraged, desperate, and at the end of her rope. But she wasn't ready to give up on her dream to work at the *World*. She just needed a new plan.

Nellie pulled herself together and borrowed a few coins from her landlady so she could take a streetcar to the newspaper district. She went right to the entrance of the *World* building, talked her way past the guard at the front door, and headed straight to the office of managing editor John Cockerill. It was a big, gutsy move.

John Cockerill knew who Nellie was, and although he was likely knee-deep in work, he agreed to meet with her on the spot and hear her out. Nellie didn't waste any time in pitching the editor a story she believed was very strong. For the article, Nellie told Cockerill she would travel to Europe and then return to America in steerage class, which was the miserable, low-fare area of a ship. By traveling in steerage, Nellie would learn firsthand how many immigrants, who typically traveled

issue; she would meet and interview top newspaper editors for their thoughts. It worked! In a matter of days Nellie was sitting in the offices of the *World*, the *Sun*, and the *Herald*, taking down the editors' words, quote by quote.

in steerage, endured the smelly, cramped, suffocating, cold, and unsanitary conditions as they crossed the Atlantic en route to the Castle Garden Port in New York. The idea was bold and the kind of human-interest story Nellie liked to tackle.

Cockerill was intrigued. He could see Nellie had spunk and drive, and he knew she could write. Even though he wasn't keen on hiring women reporters, Nellie's idea had merit. He gave her 25 dollars up front and asked her to come back after he discussed the idea with his boss, Joseph Pulitzer.

This smart move proved to be a pivotal moment in Nellie's life, and in a few days she met with Cockerill again. Although he didn't accept her steerage story, he did have another article he wanted Nellie to write. This new idea was outlandish and very risky. But it was an idea Nellie Bly couldn't resist.

TOTALLY COMMITTED

"I said I could and I would. And I did."

—NELLIE BLY

WITHOUT A lot of fanfare or fuss, John Cockerill asked Nellie if she would be willing to go undercover to Blackwell's Island, one of the largest and most notorious psychiatric hospitals for women in New York. He had received a number

Blackwell's Island Lunatic Asylum.
New York Public Library

of tips that women patients were being abused at Blackwell's. Women were committed to the asylum after a doctor or judge proclaimed them "insane." But Cockerill informed Nellie he had heard that some of the women at Blackwell's Island were sane immigrants who were treated horrendously.

To take on this investigative story, Cockerill told Nellie she would need to fake insanity and get committed to the Blackwell's asylum. For anonymity, she would need to change her name from Nellie Bly to something else.

Would she do it? Cockerill asked. Nellie said she would try. They decided on the pseudonym

Nellie practices acting "insane" in her apartment.
Wikimedia Commons PD-Art

Nellie Brown, which had her NB initials and allowed her to answer to her first name. Getting into the asylum would take ingenuity and planning, and getting out would be critical. Nellie asked Cockerill how he planned to get her out of the institution and he assured her he would find a way.

Nellie went back to her apartment to hatch a plan that would get her committed to Blackwell's Island. Step one: she needed to find a place where people would notice her. Step two: she needed to act like someone with an obvious mental problem. Step three: she needed to be committed.

Standing in front of her mirror, Nellie practiced making expressions she imagined a person with a mental illness might make. She opened her eyes as wide as possible and stared without blinking, but she wasn't quite sure how to behave. "What a difficult task, I thought, to appear before a crowd of people and convince them I was insane. I had never been near insane persons in my life, and had not the faintest idea of what their actions were like," Nellie later wrote. "I began to think my task a hopeless one; but it had to be done."

After staying awake all night reading scary ghost stories, the now tired and anxious Nellie mustered the courage to start her audacious adventure. The next morning, she put on a gray dress and looked disheveled and befuddled as she walked to a boardinghouse called the Temporary Home for Females on Second Avenue. There, the assistant matron, Irene Stenard, checked her in. Nellie had carefully chosen this home as the place to make her acting debut as a woman with a mental illness. She hoped it would be a performance that would land her where she wanted to be—the insane asylum, as it was called at the time.

After getting settled in her room, Nellie wandered down to the parlor so other boarders would see her. She sat in the back of the room and tried to look lost and upset. Every so often Nellie would blurt out that the other boarders looked crazy. "It was a wretchedly lonely evening," Nellie wrote, "and the light which fell from the solitary gas jet in the parlor, and oil-lamp [in] the hall, helped to envelop us in a dusky hue and dye our spirits navy blue." When it got late, Nellie started to act agitated, telling others she wanted to spend the night sleeping in the stairwell. Finally, a maid coaxed her to a room. Nellie forced herself to stay up the entire night and kept her mind occupied by focusing on mice and cockroaches skittering about the room.

The next day Nellie was exhausted, but her acting performance still needed a big crescendo. Cleverly, she drew a great deal of attention by refusing to leave her room and exclaiming over and over again that someone had misplaced her luggage. Eventually, Stenard called in two police officers to intervene. The officers and Stenard escorted Nellie to the nearby police station to figure out what was wrong with her. So far, it seemed like Nellie's secret plan was working.

Nellie was then taken to the Essex Market Police Court, where kindhearted Judge Duffy listened to her and tried to assess her needs. This was the third time in her life that Nellie had stood before a judge. The first time was when she was 14, defending her mother's decision to divorce John Jackson Ford. The second time was when she charged Samuel Jackson with mishandling her inheritance. This time, at 23 years old, she stood before a man who was judging her.

Judge Duffy listened to her confusing tale that seemed to be changing by the minute. She now told him that, in addition to losing her luggage, she was from Cuba. She also said she had severe headaches and was losing her memory. Concerned about the young woman, the judge sent Nellie to New York's Bellevue Hospital for further examination. He also called in reporters to see if they could find out who she was, and articles were soon published about the mysterious woman at Bellevue. The *New York Sun* ran an article headlined WHO IS THIS INSANE GIRL? The *New York Times* ran an article titled IN AND ABOUT THE CITY: A MYSTERIOUS WAIF. BELLEVUE SHELTERS A GIRL OF WHOM NOTHING IS KNOWN.

After a variety of tests were performed at Bellevue, four doctors diagnosed Nellie as insane. She was then taken in an ambulance, on a dilapidated boat, and then in another ambulance to the dreary, frightening fortress of the Blackwell's Island Insane Asylum.

As Nellie looked around at the other women in the second ambulance, she wondered if they were being unfairly driven to a prison for life. It was a discouraging sight, but Nellie had now accomplished step three: she had been committed.

SEPTEMBER 25, 1887— A LONG, HORRIBLE DAY

"The insane asylum on Blackwell's Island is a human rat-trap. It is easy to get in, but once there it is impossible to get out."
—NELLIE BLY

ALTHOUGH TIRED and undoubtedly terrified, Nellie began her work as an investigative journalist as soon as she was checked in to Blackwell's. Quietly observing her bleak surroundings, she quickly noticed that some of the women were immigrants who didn't speak English and had little chance of explaining they were not insane. The following days at Blackwell's, Nellie worked as an anonymous reporter. She took precise mental notes and described the ordeal before her. "I was to chronicle faithfully the experiences I underwent, and when once within the walls of the asylum to find out and describe its inside workings, which are always, so effectually hidden by white-capped nurses, as well as by bolts and bars, from the knowledge of the public."

The asylum staff instructed Nellie to go to the dining hall with the other patients. As she stood in line for supper, she observed that the other women looked cold, lost, and hopeless. In the dining hall, Nellie was seated on a long bench at a table with many patients. Her first meal of five prunes, stale bread with rancid butter, and pink-colored tea looked inedible—and one patient quickly snatched Nellie's bread. Nellie didn't eat anything for dinner and left the table hungry.

Later that evening, Nellie was taken into a cold, damp bathroom and ordered to undress. Nellie protested, but the nurses told her to "shut up" and forced her to remove her clothes. Nellie stepped into an ice-cold bathtub and was scrubbed down by another patient. She explained the worst was yet to come. "Suddenly I got, one after the other, three buckets of water over my head—ice-cold water, too—into my eyes, my ears, my nose and my mouth. I think I experienced some of the sensations of a drowning person as they dragged me, gasping, shivering and quaking, from the tub."

Nellie was given a simple slip to wear and ushered into a single room with a cot that might as well have been a prison cell. With wet hair and a wet slip, Nellie got into the bed, shivering. She pulled up a sheet and a wool blanket that was too short to cover her feet. As she lay in bed in the darkness, listening to the sounds of this frightening place, she heard the night nurse lock her door. Nellie started to worry. It occurred to her that if a fire broke out, escape would be impossible with bars on the windows and doors individually locked. Freezing, hungry, and anxious, Nellie stayed awake most of the night wondering what she'd gotten herself into this time. When she had to get up the next morning, her hair was still damp, and a day of heartache awaited her.

Every day at Blackwell's had a similar routine:

We were compelled to get up at 5.30 o'clock, and at 7.15 we were told to collect in the hall, where the experience of waiting, as on the evening previous, was repeated. When we got into the dining-room at last we found a bowl of cold tea, a slice of buttered bread and a saucer of oatmeal, with molasses on it, for each patient. I was hungry, but the food would not down. I asked for unbuttered bread and was given it. I cannot tell you of anything which is the same dirty, black color. It was hard, and in places nothing more than dried dough. I found a spider in my slice, so I did not eat it. I tried the oatmeal and molasses, but it was wretched, and so I en-

deavored, but without much show of success, to choke down the tea. After we were back to the sitting-room a number of women were ordered to make the beds, and some of the patients were put to scrubbing and others given different duties which covered all the work in the hall. It is not the attendants who keep the institution so nice for the poor patients, as I had always thought, but the patients, who do it all themselves—even to cleaning the nurses' bedrooms and caring for their clothing.

Nellie got to know some of the patients who were dressed in scant clothing, required to eat terrible food, forced to work, and forced to sit for hours on hard benches. Nellie carefully observed how the nurses interacted with the patients. Some nurses were kind, but others were gruff and abusive and pushed, grabbed, shoved, choked, and hit the patients.

OCTOBER 4, 1887— GOING HOME

AFTER 10 long days, Cockerill sent lawyer Peter Hendricks to release Nellie from the asylum. It wasn't easy for Nellie to say good-bye to some of the women she had befriended, but she knew her newspaper articles would shed light on the dire situation at Blackwell's and might help improve conditions.

Nellie's first article, *Behind Asylum Bars*, was published in the *World* on Sunday, October 9, 1887, followed one week later by a second article, *Inside the Madhouse*. The articles rocked the media and were picked up by newspapers across America. Nellie Bly had truly made a name for herself.

After her articles appeared, an investigation was conducted at Blackwell's, which resulted in increased funding for the asylum. Many improvements were made to provide healthier food and cleaner living conditions for the patients. In addition, some of the immigrants Nellie had written about were released from Blackwell's Island, and a number of nurses were fired.

After her undercover work on this investigative piece, Nellie published her articles in a book titled *Ten Days in a Mad-House*, published in 1887 by Ian L. Munro, Publisher in New York City.

Nellie was also hired full time at the *World*. But what would the plucky reporter do next?

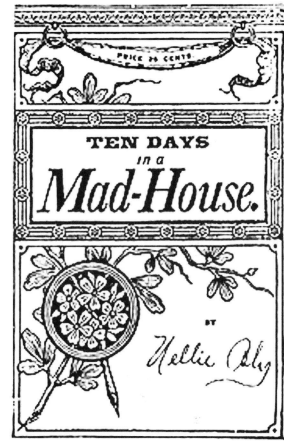

Nellie publishes a book about her experience.
Wikimedia Commons PD-Art

*

GOING GLOBAL

"I approached my editor rather timidly on the subject. I was afraid that he would think the idea too wild and visionary."

—Nellie Bly

When Nellie returned to her apartment in New York City after 10 days on Blackwell's Island, she was suddenly in the spotlight. People learned New York's "mysterious insane girl" was daredevil reporter Nellie Bly, who had single-handedly uncovered a slew of problems at the women's asylum. Many readers were impressed and eagerly looked for her byline and future stories.

With her new full-time reporting job at the *World*, Nellie's workload increased dramatically, as did the newspaper's circulation. Things were definitely looking up. Nellie buckled down and got busy, coming up with story ideas and then going out into the field to do the essential reporting and writing. With a steady income, Nellie could now afford a larger apartment in New York City; she invited her mother to move in with her.

UNDERCOVER FOR THE UNDERDOG

As a stunt reporter, Nellie wrote stories by posing as someone else and placing herself in real-life situations. Rather than reporting *on* a story, she often became part *of* the story. She needed to be part actress, part detective, and part reporter.

Today stunt reporting is frowned upon in journalism as being biased and dishonest. But in 1887, as the field of journalism was evolving, the stunt-oriented undercover approach was used. For Nellie's asylum articles, for example, she hoodwinked many people into believing she was insane. She fooled Irene Stenard and the boarders at the Temporary Home for Females. And she also fooled the police, Judge Duffy, the Bellevue Hospital doctors and nurses, various reporters, ambulance drivers, the staff at Blackwell's, and some of the mental patients. Nonetheless, her articles about the asylum were published and read and helped improve the deplorable conditions there.

Nellie was on a roll. She continued to find information for riveting newspaper stories by passing herself off as someone else. Whether she posed as a servant to shed light on ruthless employment agencies or pretended to be an unwed mother to expose individuals who sold babies, her objective was to unearth and report on the swindlers, crooks, thieves, liars, and criminals who took advantage of society's downtrodden people. Readers seemed to love it.

Nellie also wrote feature stories as herself and not as an imposter. For example, she became part of a chorus line to write about dancing on stage, she visited police court to interview women prisoners, and she wrote about unconventional communal living in New York's Oneida Community.

But one of Nellie's ideas surpassed all the rest.

THE IDEA HEARD ROUND THE WORLD

As a newspaper reporter, Nellie was adept at coming up with intriguing story ideas about unfair employment, political corruption, scandals, high-profile people, or unusual events. Her most extraordinary idea, however, was presented in the fall of 1888. Nellie asked John Cockerill if she could travel around the world faster than the character Phileas Fogg in Jules Verne's popular adventure novel *Around the World in Eighty Days*. Nellie's plan was to circumnavigate (go around) the globe in less than 80 days and write all about it.

Cockerill told Nellie her idea had already been discussed at the paper, and they had intended to send a male reporter around the world. But the editor liked the notion of sending Nellie and discussed the idea with the newspaper's business manger. The business manager, not surprisingly, was completely against it. He said Nellie had three strikes against her—she would need to be chaperoned, she would take too much luggage, and she spoke only English.

But three strikes or not, Nellie's "round the world" idea was approved about one year later. She was told to go home and pack, while staffers at the *World* began to organize her travel itinerary. For her route, Nellie would head east from Hoboken, New Jersey, and circle all the way around the globe for about 75 days to return to the United States at the Port of San Francisco, California. From San Francisco she'd cross America and return to Jersey City, New Jersey. Nellie's primary modes of transportation would be aboard a steamship or train as she traversed Earth's water or land. Her longest train rides would be from northern France to southern Italy, and from San Francisco to New Jersey.

For the bulk of her trip, Nellie would sail aboard four large steamships—the *Augusta Victoria* (from New Jersey to England, across the Atlantic Ocean), the *Victoria* (from southern Italy to Sri Lanka—across the Mediterranean Sea, Red Sea, and Arabian Sea), the *Oriental* (from Sri Lanka to Hong Kong—across the Indian Ocean, Straits of Malacca, and China Sea) and the *Oce-* *anic* (from Hong Kong to San Francisco—across the China Sea and Pacific Ocean). Her journey would include many unique stops along the way: England, France, Italy, Egypt, Sri Lanka, Singapore, Hong Kong, and Japan.

Nellie decided to pack lightly so she could travel efficiently and carry everything she needed with her. There would be no waiting for lost luggage because missing a connecting train or steamer could delay her for days. She certainly didn't want to risk it.

Without wasting a minute, Nellie headed to Fifth Avenue to have dressmakers quickly design and sew a travel gown and a lightweight summer dress she would wear for her three-month adventure. By the end of the day, Nellie had both dresses in hand. She then bought a Scotch plaid ulster [overcoat] and a handheld piece of luggage called a gripsack. In the gripsack Nellie said she crammed in

two traveling caps, three veils, a pair of slippers,
a complete outfit of toilet articles, ink-stand,
pens, pencils, and copy-paper, pins, needles
and thread, a dressing gown, a tennis blazer, a
small flask and a drinking cup, several complete
changes of underwear, a liberal supply of hand-
kerchiefs and fresh ruchings [decorative trim]
and most bulky and uncompromising of all, a
jar of cold cream to keep my face from chapping
in the varied climates I should encounter.

Nellie sets out for her daring trip around the world.
Library of Congress LC-USZ62-59923

MAKE A GREAT IDEAS BOX

NELLIE BLY HAD MANY GREAT IDEAS, which helped her succeed as a reporter and author. Having good ideas is a plus for any budding reporter, and it's smart to have a special place to keep them. When an idea for a story or article pops into your head, write it down and place it in your Great Ideas Box. Think about investigative stories you might like to write. Are there things in your world that bother you or that you'd like to change?

You'll Need

* Empty cigar box (or similar-sized cardboard box with a lid)
* Sandpaper
* Paintbrush
* Light-colored acrylic paint
* Markers
* Computer and printer (optional)
* Craft glue or glue stick
* Printer paper 8½ by 11 inches (21.6 by 28 cm)
* Ribbon (optional)
* Small pencil (optional)
* Decoupage paste (optional)

1. Find an empty cigar box and pull off any stickers. Use sandpaper to smooth out the sides of the box.

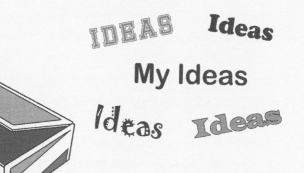

2. Paint the box with a light-colored paint and let it dry. Repaint the box about three times to cover it completely.

3. Decorate the box with the words *My Ideas* or *Ideas*, or choose your own words. You can use permanent markers and write directly on the box. Or, you can use a computer to type words in different fonts (a large font size works well) and different colors. Then print the pages, cut out the words, and glue them to the sides of your box.

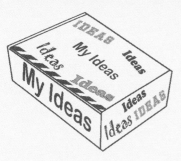

4. You may like to add ribbon to the box or glue on a small pencil as a handle.

5. You can also add a final coat of decoupage paste, which adds a shiny, lacquered finish.

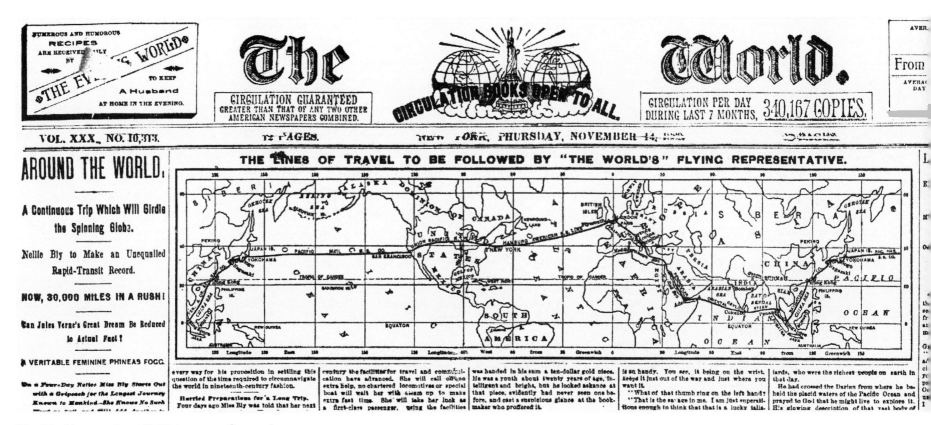

The World.

NUMEROUS AND HUMOROUS RECIPES ARE RECEIVED DAILY BY THE EVENING WORLD TO KEEP A Husband AT HOME IN THE EVENING.

CIRCULATION GUARANTEED GREATER THAN THAT OF ANY TWO OTHER AMERICAN NEWSPAPERS COMBINED.

CIRCULATION BOOKS OPEN TO ALL.

CIRCULATION PER DAY DURING LAST 7 MONTHS, 340,167 COPIES.

VOL. XXX., NO. 10,313.   12 PAGES.   NEW YORK, THURSDAY, NOVEMBER 14, 1889.

AROUND THE WORLD.

A Continuous Trip Which Will Girdle the Spinning Globe.

Nellie Bly to Make an Unequalled Rapid-Transit Record.

NOW, 30,000 MILES IN A RUSH!

Can Jules Verne's Great Dream Be Reduced to Actual Fact?

A VERITABLE FEMININE PHINEAS FOGG.

On a Four-Day Notice Miss Bly Starts Out with a Gripsack for the Longest Journey Known to Mankind—She Knows No Such ...

THE LINES OF TRAVEL TO BE FOLLOWED BY "THE WORLD'S" FLYING REPRESENTATIVE.

The *World* mapped out Nellie's voyage for readers. Library of Congress

Nellie didn't have room to bring the summer dress she'd just purchased, and she chose not to bring a gun, which some folks recommended.

On the bright Thursday morning of November 14, 1889, Nellie Bly waved good-bye to friends from the deck of her steamship, the *Augusta Victoria*, at the Hoboken Pier in New Jersey. As the whistle blew and the ship set sail across the Atlantic Ocean to England, Nellie worried about severe weather and shipwrecks but tried to be brave. "I felt lost. My head felt dizzy and my heart felt as if it would burst," Nellie wrote. "Only seventy-five days! Yes, but it seemed an age and the world lost its roundness and seemed a long distance with no end, and—well, I never turn back."

And she didn't turn back. The sea was rough the first day of travel; Nellie suffered from seasickness and was unable to keep food down. Exhausted, she slept from 7:00 in the evening until

Nellie begins her journey aboard the *Augusta Victoria* steamer. Wikimedia Commons PD-US

4:30 the next afternoon. But when she awoke that afternoon, she was famished and was finally able to eat a large dinner.

To pass the time on the weeklong voyage to England, Nellie enjoyed meeting other passengers and watching the antics of a terrier named Homie. After the ship docked at Southampton, England, Nellie was greeted by a male chaperone who helped her board a train to London. Nellie was cold and hungry as she and her escort took a horse-drawn carriage to the London-based office of the *World* newspaper to pick up her passport. Passing through the unfamiliar streets, Nellie caught a glimpse of landmarks such as Westminster Abbey, the Houses of Parliament, and the Thames River.

Nellie then took a train to her next connection and finally had a moment to rest. "I slept an easy, happy sleep, filled with dreams of home until I was waked by the train stopping," she wrote. Then it was time to cross the English Channel and board another train for Nellie's first grand adventure in Amiens, France—meeting author Jules Verne.

MEETING JULES VERNE

THE TRAIN ride to France was uneventful, but Nellie was full of eager anticipation. Special arrangements had been made for Nellie to meet the famous author Jules Verne, whose book had inspired her to travel around the world. At the train station in Amiens, France, where Jules Verne now lived, Nellie was greeted by Mr. Verne, his wife, and a journalist from Paris. The journalist would translate the Vernes' French language to English.

Nellie and her London chaperone were then escorted to the Vernes's home, where everyone had a chance to chat in a large sitting room with a fire crackling in the fireplace and a cordial snack of wine with biscuits. Nellie asked Verne where he got the idea for *Around the World in Eighty Days*, and he explained it was from an article he had read in a French newspaper. After a quick visit to the author's study, it was time for Nellie to be on her way to continue her own race around the world. The celebrated novelist gave Nellie kindhearted encouragement and enthusiastically wished her tremendous success on her voyage. Without delay, Nellie was soon heading to southern Italy.

WORLD CONNECTIONS

NELLIE WAS a prolific and conscientious writer during her international travels. She wrote about the ships and trains she rode on, the people she met, food she ate, weather she encountered, places she explored, and the customs and events of different lands. As a reliable foreign correspondent, she sent letters and articles to the

World as often as she could. Unfortunately, her letters didn't get to the paper in a timely manner and John Cockerill wouldn't hear from her for weeks. To keep readers interested in Nellie's journey, the *World* wrote articles and updates about the places she visited. The paper also cleverly created a contest and asked readers to guess the exact day and time Nellie would return home. The winner would get a free trip to Europe. America was spellbound by Nellie's journey, and the contest forms flooded in.

After leaving Jules Verne's home, Nellie boarded a train at 1:30 in the morning for a long and somewhat tedious two-day train ride through the French and Italian countryside to the southern port of Brindisi, Italy. At one stop Nellie stepped outside, and her descriptive writing skills came to life. "I went out on the platform, and the fog seemed to lift for an instant, and I saw on one side a beautiful beach and a smooth bay dotted with boats bearing oddly-shaped and brightly-colored sails, which somehow looked to me like mammoth butterflies, dipping, dipping about in search of honey."

Nellie had been on her world trek for about 10 days now, and she knew that back in the States, friends and family were preparing Thanksgiving menus of turkey, stuffing, mashed potatoes, cranberries, and pumpkin pie.

In Brindisi, Nellie boarded the *Victoria* steamer that took her south through the Medi-

Visionary Jules Verne

FAMOUS SCIENCE FICTION writer Jules Verne took readers on fantastic voyages around the world, to the Moon, far below the sea, and even to the center of the Earth.

His curiosity about life was ignited early on. Born in the bustling seaport of Nantes, France, in 1828, Verne's family home was located on a small island on the town's Loire River. He was constantly surrounded by water, ships, and sailors. Nantes was an exciting place to grow up and sparked Verne's extraordinary imagination. He also loved reading adventure books such as Daniel Defoe's novel *Robinson Crusoe.*

As a young man, Verne first followed in his father's footsteps and moved to Paris to study law. But deep down, he was drawn to something else—writing. Unable to put his pen down, he began to write poems, short stories, and plays. Writing eventually became his livelihood.

Science fiction writer Jules Verne.
Wikimedia Commons PD-Art

Verne had a wonderful knack for weaving science, math, and geography into the story lines of his futuristic novels. He enchanted readers with classic novels, including: *Five Weeks in a Balloon, From the Earth to the Moon, A Journey to the Center of the Earth*, and *Twenty Thousand Leagues Under the Sea.*

His classic 1873 adventure novel, *Around the World in Eighty Days*, was the inspiration for Nellie Bly's exciting world voyage and book, *Nellie Bly's Book: Around the World in Seventy-Two Days.*

terranean Sea. After a few days, the ship stopped at Port Said of Egypt, a coaling station where the ship would refuel with coal. This stop gave Nellie a chance to explore a new city, but it proved to be upsetting. As the *Victoria* anchored, many beggars tried to board the ship, and passengers thoughtlessly used walking canes and umbrellas to swat the beggars away. Nellie didn't like what she witnessed and wrote, "a stick beats more ugliness into a person than it ever beats out."

In Port Said there was time for a short stopover. Nellie saw young Egyptian boys offering rides on burros, calling out, "Here's Gladstone! Take a ride; see Gladstone with two beautiful black eyes." Nellie enjoyed a burro ride, and there was also time to browse through a few shops and listen to music before getting back on the ship.

ENCHANTING TROPICS

AFTER COALING, the *Victoria* traveled south on the Red Sea and eventually stopped in the Port of Aden in the southern part of the Arabian Peninsula. Here the weather was hot and balmy, but it didn't seem to bother Nellie. For about seven hours, Nellie explored the exotic town like a tourist and was impressed with the Adenites' bright white teeth, lime-bleached yellow hair, and colorful jewelry. She paid for a carriage ride around the small town, and back at the pier watched Somali boys gracefully swim in the nearby waters and dive for coins cheerfully tossed by passengers on the ship.

Nellie then reboarded the ship for the journey to Colombo, Sri Lanka. When she arrived in scenic, tree-lined Colombo, Nellie immediately sent a cable to the *World* to update her editor on where she was and how she was doing.

Like a curious sightseer, Nellie took time to poke around the city of Colombo and visit places such as the ornate Grand Oriental Hotel. In the hotel, she sat in a large wicker chair surrounded by tropical flowers, sipped a cool, lime beverage, and enjoyed a curry shrimp dish. She also had her first ride on a jinricksha (rickshaw), a small two-wheel cart pulled by a man.

In Sri Lanka, Nellie was to board her next ship, the *Oriental*, which would take her 3,500 miles across the seas to Hong Kong. Unfortunately, the Colombo stop was delayed five days waiting for another ship to come in. Nellie became anxious and angry, fearing she would lose valuable time on her race around the world. Finally, the *Oriental* set sail for the two-week voyage toward Hong Kong. Nellie was happy to be moving forward again and enjoyed her next stops in Penang, and the country of Singapore.

Whether it was due to travel fatigue or impatience, Nellie's temper was starting to flare. Nellie liked to stay up late and sleep in, and she became irritated when squabbling children on the ship woke her too early in the morning. But her grouchy mood didn't stop her from exploring Singapore, where she threw caution to the wind and bought herself a new "friend" in the form of a little monkey she named McGinty. Nellie took her new pet on board the *Oriental*, which made good time sailing toward Hong Kong, even though the vessel had to surge through raging monsoon rains and enormous ocean swells. Although Nellie got a kick out of how the ship was tossed high and low over the waves, many passengers became seasick or slipped and fell on the deck.

A SHOCK IN HONG KONG

IT WAS now late December, and the *Oriental* arrived in Hong Kong two days early. Taking a look at her newest destination, Nellie wrote, "Hong Kong is strangely picturesque. It is a terraced city, the terraces being formed by the castle-like, arcaded buildings perched tier after tier up the mountain's verdant side. The regularity with which the houses are built in rows made me wildly fancy them a gigantic staircase, each stair made in imitation of castles."

Nellie was thrilled with the early arrival. She raced to the offices of the Oriental and Occidental Steamship Company to find out how soon she could head to her next stop of Japan and continue making good time on her race around the world. But her mood quickly soured when the office clerk at the steamship

Nellie sometimes traveled by rickshaw.
Library of Congress LC-USZ62-118508

company gave her shocking and confusing news. With only about one month left of her travels, Nellie learned—to her dismay—that a reporter from *Cosmopolitan Magazine* named Elizabeth Bisland was also racing around the world in an attempt to beat her! Elizabeth had left the same day Nellie set out around the world, but this reporter traveled west around the globe while Nellie traveled east.

Nellie tried to comprehend what she was hearing. First there was confusion and disbelief, followed by indignation. After all her hard work, it must have felt like a rotten trick. But Nellie wasn't going to let the news get her down.

"I promised my editor that I would go around the world in seventy-five days, and if I accomplish that I shall be satisfied," Nellie wrote.

Her spirit was strong and she was determined to beat Phileas Fogg's record, meet her 75-day goal, and hopefully finish before Elizabeth Bisland. But questions raced through her mind. *Would she have more unexpected delays? Would the weather slow her down? Would she meet her goal?*

That night Nellie had a few dinner invitations but declined the offers and chose to eat by herself. The next day while exploring Hong Kong, Nellie was busy. She watched a pretty marriage procession adorned with elegant Chinese lanterns, attended a theatrical production of *Ali Baba and the Forty Thieves*, and visited Victoria Peak, the highest point on the island.

On Christmas Eve, Nellie set out on a smaller boat for the town of Canton, which was not far from Hong Kong. This was a very special time for her. She loved sitting alone on the quiet deck in complete darkness and looking up at the many glistening stars. As the boat moved through the water, Nellie listened to the gentle lapping of the waves, which she found peaceful and soothing. She started to think about the holiday season back home: the Christmas tree, gift giving, delicious foods, and being with her family.

The next day, December 25, was a fascinating but troubling experience for Nellie. Her first stop in Canton was to visit an execution ground, a jail, and a torture chamber, which she was very curious to see and grateful to leave. She was also able to tour a Chinese temple called the Temple of the Five Hundred Gods and an examination room for Chinese students known as the Hall of Auspicious Stars. There was a lot more to see. Nellie was saddened by a visit to a leper colony, she had lunch at the Temple of the Dead, and she marveled at an ancient water clock.

It had been a long, hectic day in Canton and a Christmas Nellie would never forget. She was glad to be back on the boat to Hong Kong again to visit with McGinty and think about the days ahead.

ONE MONTH TO THE FINISH LINE

At last it was time for Nellie to leave Hong Kong and board her final steamship, the *Oceanic*, for a five-day sail to Yokohama, Japan. Nellie celebrated New Year's Eve with some of the passengers, and it was a festive evening of music, games, and enjoying oysters with champagne. At midnight passengers sang "Auld Lang Syne" to usher in the first day of 1890.

Being in Japan was a treat for Nellie. She was enchanted by how pristine and beautiful Yokohama looked and said it had a "cleaned-up Sunday appearance." She stayed at the Grand Hotel in town and was enamored with the Japanese women's elegant silk kimonos and sandals held up by two five-inch pieces of wood.

Nellie went with friends to the city of Kamakura, which was about 16 miles from Yokohama. She wanted to see the famous 50-foot-high bronze statue of the Buddha called the Daibutsu. This was a rare treat as Nellie described it: "The face is eight feet long, the eye is four feet, the ear six feet six and one-half inches, the nose three feet eight and one-half inches, the mouth is three feet two and one-half inches, the diameter of the lap is thirty-six feet, and the circumference of the thumb is over three feet. I had my photograph taken sitting on its thumb with two friends."

Later in the day Nellie saw a beautiful fan tree and lotus pond, and had a bite to eat at a teahouse. Nellie's visit to Japan was one of the most memorable parts of her world journey and an experience she cherished. Then it was time to board the *Oceanic* to cross the great Pacific for 5,000 miles and head home. Nellie had mixed feelings as she stood on the deck of the ship, waving good-bye with her handkerchief. "My feverish eagerness to be off again on my race around the world was strongly mingled with regret at leaving such charming friends and such a lovely land."

As Nellie sailed back to San Francisco in the United States, she was desperate to move fast and make good time. The chief engineer of the ship, Mr. Allen, wrote this motivational couplet on paper and placed it throughout the ship's engine room.

For Nellie Bly
We'll win or die.
January 20, 1890

When the boat was nearing San Francisco, Nellie learned that a terrible snowstorm had hit the United States and would slow down her train ride across the country. She was horrified. Fortunately, the *World* chartered a special train that took her through southern states that didn't have snow and then up to Chicago, where she caught a few more trains to her final destination in New Jersey.

ZIPPING ACROSS THE CONTINENT

From San Francisco to the many stops along the way, people cheered Nellie on. Excited well-wishers came out by the hundreds to see her. They shouted, "There's Nellie Bly!" "Hurray for Nellie Bly!"

Nellie was both delighted and overwhelmed. "I only remember my trip across the continent as one maze of happy greetings, happy wishes, congratulating telegrams, fruit, flowers, loud cheers, wild hurrahs, rapid hand-shaking and a beautiful car filled with fragrant flowers attached to a swift engine that was tearing like

The Daibutsu statue of Buddha.
Library of Congress LC-DIG-ppmsca-31358

mad through flower-dotted valley and over snow-tipped mountain, on–on–on!" Nellie wrote. "It was glorious!"

On Saturday, January 25, 1890, thousands of people flocked to the train station in Jersey City, New Jersey, to greet her. As people cheered and cannons boomed, Nellie jumped down from the train to the platform and raised her cap high.

With a final world-breaking record of 72 days, 6 hours, 11 minutes, and 14 seconds, she had beaten the fictional Phileas Fogg and the real-life Elizabeth Bisland. But most of all, she was happy to be finally home again.

BACK TO WORK

THERE WAS no time to rest. Nellie needed to get to work, because America was eagerly waiting to read her words. Her first article, *Father Time Outdone*, was published in the *World* the day after she returned home, and more articles about her travels appeared over the following weeks. The winner of the Nellie Bly guessing game was "F. W. Stevens" from New York City, who came incredibly close to her record time and beat out thousands of other contestants.

Nellie was clearly a celebrity and perhaps the most famous woman in the world at this time. Her fame brought added income. She was asked to speak about her world adventures to sold-out audiences, and her name and image were used to sell merchandise such as a popular board game that hit the shelves. That same year, she compiled her articles for a book titled *Nellie Bly's Book: Around the World in Seventy-Two Days*, published by the Pictorial Weeklies Company in New York City.

But it wasn't all fun and games. Nellie knew her trip around the world had increased the

Nellie makes it home!

DESIGN A BOARD GAME

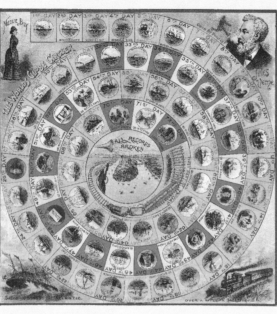

After Nellie returned home, a board game called Round the World with Nellie Bly was created.

The University of Iowa Libraries, Iowa City, Iowa

1. Choose a theme for your game. Will your players go around your town, school, neighborhood, or somewhere else? Give your game a catchy title.

2. Use a ruler and pencil to draw a 20-by-20-inch (50.8-by-50.8-cm) square on the poster board. Cut out the square to use as your game board.

3. Trace over the circle on this page to make a pattern. Use it to trace 30 circles on your pieces of printer paper. Cut out the 30 circles.

4. Use a marker to write *Day 1*, *Day 2*, *Day 3*, and so on, within each circle.

When Nellie traveled around the world, the *New York World* newspaper created a game called "Round the World with Nellie Bly" to hook readers into her journey. Create your own board game using the theme of getting around somewhere in 30 days.

You'll Need

* Ruler
* Pencil
* Poster board 22 by 28 inches (55.9 by 71.1 cm)
* Scissors
* 3 to 4 sheets of white paper, 8½ by 11 inches (21.6 by 28 cm)
* Circle pattern (2¼-inch [5.7 cm] diameter circle)
* Marker (fine or medium tip)
* Craft glue or glue stick
* 4 small rounded stones (game pieces)
* Paint (4 different colors)
* Paintbrush
* Decorative images or graphics (optional)
* One die

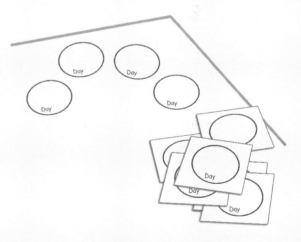

DESIGN A BOARD GAME—CONTINUED

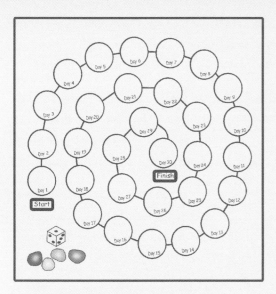

5. Arrange the circles on the game board in a spiral to create a path.

6. Glue the circles to your game board. Draw a line to connect the circles.

7. Write *Start* below Day 1 and *Finish* below Day 30.

8. Paint each of the four small stones a different color.

9. Now, it's up to you to design how to play your game! Think about simple rules to follow. Decide where a player starts and ends. Maybe players start at your home and their goal is to get to a movie. Maybe they finish at your home.

10. In various "day" circles, write in a place that fits your theme, such as a skate park, theater, or library. You don't need places for every day.

11. Also, in various "day" circles, write in commands such as *Move ahead three days*, *Go back five days*, *Go to the rec center*, or *Stay put*. You don't need commands for every day.

12. Decorate your game board with colors, images, or graphics.

13. Play the game by yourself first. This will be a helpful test run to make sure your game works.

14. Now, with two, three, or four players, roll the die and begin the game. The first person to get to the finish wins!

World's circulation, which meant more money for the paper. When she didn't receive a raise or even a bonus for her 72 days of globe-trotting, she angrily quit her job at the paper.

After being in the limelight, Nellie's life started to unravel over the next three years. It was a difficult and depressing time, and at one point she was bedridden. She was hired on a contractual basis to write fictional pieces for a publication called the *New York Family Story Paper*, but Nellie didn't excel at this type of writing and the work soon ended. Her brother Charles died in 1890, and Nellie turned her attention toward helping take care of his two young children. Wanting to live in a more rural setting, Mary Jane leased a farm in White Plains, New York, which wasn't too far from the city. Nellie often spent weekends with her there. The farm had an orchard, fields, chickens, a cow, a horse, and dogs, and Nellie liked being outdoors, interacting with the animals and planting crops. But she still felt disconnected from her career. She reached out and wrote a letter to her former *Dispatch* colleague, Erasmus Wilson. Ever the good friend, Erasmus wrote back and encouraged Nellie to have hope and not give up.

Fortunately, in 1893, Morrill Goddard became the new editor for the *World*'s Sunday edition and had new visions for the paper. He immediately contacted Nellie and asked her to return as a reporter. Nellie realized this newspaper was a great place to be and rejoined the staff after being away for three years.

Nellie's first article after her return was a hit. On September 17, 1893, Nellie landed the front-page headline NELLIE BLY AGAIN. SHE INTERVIEWS EMMA GOLDMAN AND OTHER ANARCHISTS. For the story, Nellie visited The Tombs jail in Manhattan and interviewed 25-year-old Goldman for two hours. Goldman, a political activist, was serving time for alleged inflammatory, antigovernment protest speeches. Although many people decried Goldman as a riot-inciting agitator, Nellie's article gave a more extensive and personal view of the young woman she called a "modern Joan of Arc."

Nellie also started a new column titled *Nellie Bly's Column*, where she wrote opinion pieces about everyday life. The topics were more commonplace than compelling; Nellie wrote about having a dog as a pet, horse racing, or listening to bells on cable cars. The column wasn't that popular and was eventually dropped. Morrill Goddard encouraged Nellie to do what she did best—conduct interviews and write investigative pieces. She took his advice, and one of her next pieces changed her life.

In the summer of 1894, Nellie traveled to Chicago, Illinois, to write about a violent strike that nearly shut down the entire US train system. Thousands of factory workers who built sleeping cars for the Pullman Palace

Anarchist Emma Goldman.
Library of Congress LC-DIG-ppmsca-02894

Car Company were incredibly angry about recent salary cuts. To fight for their rights, the workers launched a nationwide strike. Federal troops were called in, and the strike turned violent and bloody.

Nellie had traveled in a number of Pullman train cars during her life, and she was initially against the strikers' position. But she wanted to know the inside story of what was happening and the strikers' demands. She interviewed strikers and their family members to get their points of view. She heard about how workers felt forced to live in the company's industrial community called Pullman town and how their meager earnings could not cover everyday living expenses. Nellie was shocked to find the Pullman town had a pretty facade that hid rows of tenement houses and poverty. She also interviewed Illinois's governor John P. Altgeld, who was against the use of federal troops to control the strikers.

The next year she traveled to Illinois to interview labor activist Eugene V. Debs, who helped found the American Railroad Union, when he was serving time in jail. Over the next months Nellie continued writing numerous articles for the *World*.

Nellie's impressive coverage of the Pullman strike got her noticed at the *Chicago Times-Herald* newspaper, which offered her a job. She took the job, left the *World*, and moved to Chicago in February 1895. At the same time, Nellie was also being wooed by a very unlikely suitor.

MARRYING A MILLIONAIRE

NELLIE'S NEW job didn't last long. In Chicago she met bachelor Robert Livingston Seaman, a New York millionaire who was temporarily in town on business. Robert owned the Brooklyn-based Iron Clad Manufacturing Company, which produced large metal milk containers.

After a few weeks, Nellie hastily married Robert on April 5, 1895, in Chicago and then moved back to New York to be with him. She was nearly 31 at the time; Robert was 70. It certainly didn't seem like a match made in heaven, and nasty rumors started to fly.

Critics wondered if this impulsive marriage to an older man was one of Nellie's clever stunts. Robert's family accused Nellie of marrying him for his money. And Robert—who became jealous of his pretty, young wife—started to

Pullman strikers line up outside the Arcade Building in Chicago. Wikimedia CommonsLibrary of Congress LC-USZ61-2126

have Nellie followed by one of his caretakers. It wasn't a peaceful first year of marriage.

Nellie turned her attention toward writing again and discovered that editors were leaving and reporters were being replaced at the *World*. Staff reporter Arthur Brisbane became the new editor for the *World*'s Sunday edition. Arthur liked Nellie and asked her to return to the newspaper and write under her famous Nellie Bly byline. Nellie accepted his offer and produced

Nellie married millionaire
Robert Livingston Seaman in 1895.

MAKE A WRITER'S BLOCK

JOURNALISTS SPEND a great deal of time writing, meeting deadlines, and finishing pieces. They need to put words down on paper on a regular basis.

But it's not uncommon for writers to experience writer's block and feel stuck. Suddenly, their ideas have dried up, words aren't flowing, and the blank paper remains blank.

For this activity, make a "writer's block" to help motivate your writing.

You'll Need

* 2-inch (5.1 cm) wood block (available at craft stores)
* Sandpaper
* Light-colored acrylic paint
* Paintbrush
* Pencil or pen
* Writing paper
* Markers
* Decoupage paste (optional)

1. Remove any stickers from the wood block and sand it lightly.

2. Paint the wood with a light-colored acrylic paint. Repaint the block two or three times to cover it completely.

3. Think about activities or behaviors that get your ideas flowing. Write a list of about six to eight short activities that would inspire you to start writing. Examples might be: "take a walk," "listen to music," "meditate," or "read."

4. With permanent markers, write six of your phrases on the block, one on each side. Create designs around your phrases.

5. You can paint the block with decoupage paste for a final coat.

6. Now set the block in a visible place. When your words need to flow, look at your writer's block and think about and practice ways to start writing again.

some of her best pieces during this time, including an insightful interview with famous women's suffragist Susan B. Anthony.

NEW BEGINNINGS

ALTHOUGH NELLIE was still busy writing and reporting, her life changed dramatically with marriage. Suddenly she was a wealthy socialite living in posh, expensive homes. In 1896 she left the *World*—yet again—and moved to Europe with Robert. She started a new chapter in her life and put her writing on hold. But after three years living in cities such as Paris, Vienna, Rome, and London, the couple returned to New York City to reorganize the Iron Clad Manufacturing Company. Nellie became president of Iron Clad, and her new focus was the world of business and the manufacture of products.

Soon tragedy struck. In 1904, after only nine years of marriage, Nellie's husband was hit by a horse and wagon while crossing the street and died one month later. Nellie's beloved younger sister, Catherine, had also died a few years earlier. To cope with her losses, Nellie threw herself into her work at Iron Clad and initiated many positive changes. Employees were given weekly paychecks, and a recreation center, eating hall, library, and small hospital were built for workers. Nellie invented and patented a number of products. She also designed and patented a nonleaking 55-gallon steel barrel for the transport of oil and gasoline.

About five years after Robert Seaman died, Nellie realized Iron Clad was losing money even though the company appeared to be thriving. She discovered employees were stealing from her, which sent her into years of complicated legal battles with dishonest workers and creditors wanting to be paid. Nellie was forced to sell Iron Clad and settle her debts.

In the summer of 1914, Nellie made arrangements for a three-week trip to Austria to resolve some of her ongoing financial problems. Even though Austria had just declared war on Serbia at the start of World War I (July 28, 1914), Nellie boarded the *Oceanic* steamship and set sail for Europe. In Austria, Nellie was in a unique position to write as a war correspondent. She contacted Arthur Brisbane, who was now an editor at the *World*'s competing paper, the *New York Evening Journal*, owned by newspaper giant William Randolph Hearst. Nellie was given the green light to write articles for the *Journal* from the front lines of World War I. The hardworking reporter was writing again.

World War 1 ended on November 11, 1918. Nellie's original three-week jaunt to Austria

Nellie became president of the Iron Clad Manufacturing Company. Carnegie Library of Pittsburgh

had lasted five years, and when she returned to New York in 1919 she encountered heartbreaking news. Her mother had died and given the bulk of Nellie's savings and property to her older brother Albert.

Now discouraged and with very little money, Nellie found regular work as a columnist for the *Journal* in 1919. Once again, her words inspired readers. Although Nellie never had children, at this later time in her life she directed her efforts toward helping struggling mothers find work and orphans find homes.

Over the next few years Nellie's health declined, and, suffering from pneumonia, she died on January 27, 1922, at the age of 57. The next day her longtime friend and colleague Arthur Brisbane wrote a beautiful tribute to Nellie in the *Journal* saying, "Nellie Bly was the best reporter in America."

Nellie accomplished a great deal in her life and helped lead the way for future journalists.

Nellie worked hard to get ahead in the male-dominated world of journalism in the late 1800s and early 1900s.

Library of Congress
LC-DIG-ds-02106

THE CHANGING WORLD OF JOURNALISM

"It's not what you look at that matters, it's what you see."

—Henry David Thoreau

From print to broadcast to the digital world of the Web today, the field of journalism has changed dramatically over the years.

When Nellie Bly was first hired at the *Pittsburgh Dispatch* in 1885, there were very few women reporters. Once hired, Nellie's instincts were to write about what she thought was unfair or wrong in the world. She had natural muckraking tendencies, the wisdom to know an important story when she saw one, and she cared about the underdog. Readers were intrigued by her stories, and she helped increase newspaper readership and sales. Her editors, George Madden at the *Dispatch*, John Cockerill at the *World*, and Arthur Brisbane at the *Journal*, knew readers enjoyed her provocative, opinionated, and sensational style.

Her reporting as a stunt journalist helped pave the way for future forms of investigative journalism.

But, when Nellie was about 30 years old, one style of journalism caused problems for readers as well as reporters.

YELLOW JOURNALISM

IN THE 1890s and early 1900s, the newspaper industry was booming in the United States. The sale of dailies thrived during this era. At the time, there were nearly 50 daily newspapers in New York City offered as morning, afternoon, and evening editions.

Technical advances in the printing press enabled newspapers to be mass produced, and mass media was exciting big business. But in 1895 as thousands of pages rapidly rolled off the presses, and as more and more readers subscribed to newspapers for their news, a bitter rivalry was brewing in New York City that started a writing style known as yellow journalism. The rivalry took place between seasoned newspaper publisher Joseph Pulitzer and young newspaper publisher William Randolph Hearst who began to battle over readership and subscriptions. Each publisher vied to have the biggest, best paper.

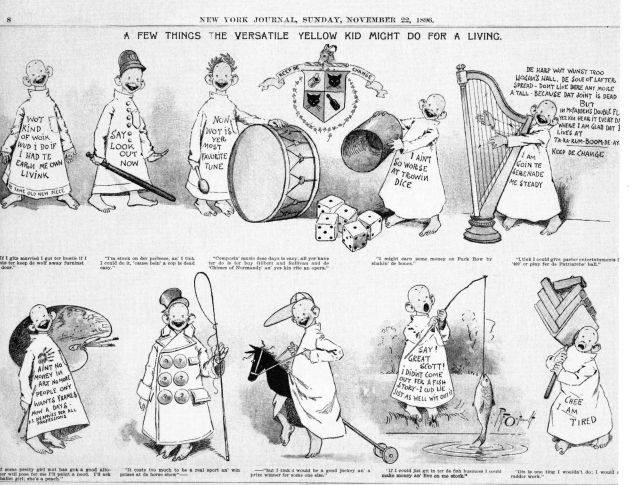

The Yellow Kid. San Francisco Academy of Comic Art Collection, The Ohio State University Billy Ireland Cartoon Library & Museum

"DIS IS GRATE STUFF"

By 1895, Pulitzer had already been running the *New York World* and competing with many other New York newspapers for nearly 12 years. To bump up *World* sales, Pulitzer hired talented cartoonist Richard Felton Outcault, who came up with *Hogan's Alley*, the first commercially successful newspaper comic strip. *Hogan's Alley*'s most unforgettable character was Mickey Dugan, a bald-headed little guy from the New York City slums who had lost his hair from lice treatments. Mickey always wore a long yellow nightshirt, which quickly earned him the nickname, "The Yellow Kid." The round-eared fellow had a perpetual grin and spoke in a New York City dialect with catchy phrases such as, "Say, dis is grate stuff," "Well hully gee, here's to you," and "Tanks awfully." Readers loved it.

Also in 1895, William Randolph Hearst arrived in New York City and acquired the *New York Morning Journal*, which he renamed the *New York Journal*. Hearst's new paper was in direct competition with Pulitzer's top-selling *New York World*.

To compete with Pulitzer's paper, Hearst needed to make the *Journal* different and highly appealing for readers. He sold his paper for the low rate of one penny, which was 50 percent cheaper than Pulitzer's two-cent paper. Hearst also hired away many of Pulitzer's key people

Joseph Pulitzer (1847–1911)

Joseph Pulitzer. Library of Congress LC-USZ62-49254

JOSEPH PULITZER was born in Mako, Hungary, in 1847. Pulitzer immigrated to the United States at the end of the Civil War and enlisted for one year in the Lincoln Calvary. After the war ended in 1865, he traveled to St. Louis and studied the English language, American law, and writing. In 1878, Pulitzer bought the *St. Louis Post-Dispatch* newspaper, which launched his publishing career. At the paper he worked tirelessly and published populist stories that exposed wrongdoing and appealed to readers' sense of justice for workers, immigrants, and the poor.

In 1883, Pulitzer bought the *New York World* and moved to New York City. Once again, he appealed to readers with stories about crime and corruption that often featured staged stunts, Nellie Bly-style, and eye-catching illustrations. Pulitzer was subject to personal attacks, and suffering from poor health, near blindness, and hearing problems, he left the newsroom at the *World* in 1890 while continuing to remain publisher of the paper.

Over the following years Pulitzer was drawn into sensational yellow journalism to sell newspapers, but he eventually made editorial changes at the *World* that reflected a more objective, truthful form of newspaper writing.

Joseph Pulitzer died in 1911; he was one of the world's most acclaimed journalists. In his will, he donated money to Columbia University in New York to help establish its school of journalism, which was founded in 1912. Five years later, in 1917, Columbia University organized the Pulitzer Prizes, which recognize achievement in newspaper journalism, literature, music, and drama, and still do today.

William Randolph Hearst (1863–1951)

WILLIAM RANDOLPH Hearst was born in San Francisco, California, in 1863. He attended Harvard University and worked on the *Harvard Lampoon* publication, but did not graduate from the school.

In 1887, when Hearst was 24 years old, he took over the *San Francisco Examiner*, previously owned by his wealthy father, George Hearst, who had made millions in mining. William Hearst transformed the *Examiner* so it offered readers investigative articles that exposed social reform topics such as municipal and corporate corruption in an eye-catching, sensational style that was popular at the time. Readership for his first paper grew.

Hearst had great aspirations in the newspaper business. In 1895 he entered the fiercely competitive world of the New York press by buying the *New York Morning Journal*. The *Journal* gained readership via its talented reporters, low-cost, and tantalizing graphics and articles readers found hard to resist.

William Randolph Hearst. LC-USZ62-68945

In addition to a career in publishing, Hearst had political aspirations. He was elected to the House of Representatives in 1902 and 1904 as a New York Democrat. From 1905 to 1910 he ran unsuccessfully for mayor of New York City twice, governor of New York, and lieutenant governor of New York.

Hearst went on to become a publishing giant, owning many newspapers and magazines. He built a castle in San Simeon, California, which was donated to California in 1957. Hearst Castle is now a California Historical Landmark open to visitors. Today Hearst Corporation is a multinational mass media group headquartered in Hearst Tower in New York City.

from the *World*, including editors Morrill Goddard and Arthur Brisbane. Hearst even convinced cartoonist Richard Outcault to join the *Journal* staff and bring along the Yellow Kid. From 1896 to 1898, Outcault illustrated The Yellow Kid in various comic series for Hearst including *McFadden's Row of Flats*, *Around the World with the Yellow Kid*, and *Ryan's Arcade*.

Pulitzer fought back. Not to be outdone by Hearst, Pulitzer hired a new cartoonist named George B. Luks to continue creating a similar "Yellow Kid" comic strip at the *World*.

The competition between Hearst and Pulitzer became dramatic and led to a sensational reporting style known as yellow journalism, named for its association with the Yellow Kid cartoon character.

Yellow journalism featured eye-catching graphics; big, bold headlines; and exaggerated, sensational stories (often about crime, sex, and violence) to dazzle readers and grab their attention.

It sold newspapers. But at what price?

A MEDIA-DRIVEN WAR?

WHEN HEARST first published the *Journal* in 1895, Cuba was struggling for its independence from Spain during the Cuban War of Independence (1895–1898). The Cuban freedom fighters waged a tough battle against the Spaniards

CREATE A CHARACTER AND COMIC STRIP

THE *HOGAN'S ALLEY* COMIC STRIP character Mickey Dugan was called the Yellow Kid. He earned his nickname because he wore a long yellow nightgown. Many comic strip characters are defined by something they wear.

For this activity, come up with your own comic strip character (human, animal, extraterrestrial, etc.) that gets its name from something it wears. Then write a simple story line to create your own comic strip.

You'll Need

* Pencil
* Writing paper
* Card stock
* Ruler
* Scissors
* Printer paper, 8½ by 11 inches (21.6 by 28 cm)
* Colored pencils or markers

1. Think about something eye-catching your main character could wear. It could be oversized shoes, bold eyeglasses, a colorful cap, suspenders, a shirt, or a crazy-looking hairstyle. It's OK to exaggerate.

2. Come up with a catchy name for your character, which could also be the title of your comic strip.

3. Next, imagine how your character might behave and write a short list of engaging character traits.

Maybe your character tells funny jokes, solves mysteries, is into sports, or likes to travel. It's up to you.

4. Create one or two different characters who could interact with your main character, and give each character a name and description.

5. Now, think about a simple story line for your main character. Read other comic strips to get an idea of how stories are told. A simple story could pose a problem for your main character, which he or she then addresses or solves.

6. To create your comic strip, use a ruler and pencil to draw a panel that is about 5 inches (12.7 cm) wide by 3 inches (7.6 cm) tall on the card stock. Cut out the template.

7. Place your printer paper horizontally and use your panel as a pattern to draw four panels on the page (two across the top, two across the bottom).

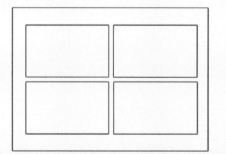

8. In each panel sketch a picture of your main character in a situation. To tell your story, think about the beginning as the first panel, the middle as the second two panels, and the end as the last panel. Note: You can also draw more than four panels if you like.

9. Use word balloons for your characters' dialogue and thought balloons for your characters' unspoken thoughts.

10. Add color to your comic strip with colored pencils or markers.

Pulitzer and Hearst shown in Yellow Kid attire in this *Puck* magazine cartoon about the 1898 Spanish-American War. Library of Congress LC-USZC4-3800

ering these wartime events, and *Journal* readers were often outraged by what they perceived was happening in Cuba.

Many newspapers across America deplored yellow journalism and did not utilize this sensational, overstated style in their coverage of the news or the conflict in Cuba. But Hearst and Pulitzer stuck with the riveting reporting style; it sold papers.

In 1898, the newspaper drama rose to new heights when US President William McKinley (25th president, from 1897 to 1901) sent the *USS Maine* battleship to Cuba's Havana Harbor in late January. McKinley was concerned about the escalating tensions between Spain and Cuba, economic interests with Cuba, and the safety of Americans on the island.

About two weeks after arriving at the harbor, the USS *Maine* mysteriously blew up and sank, killing 266 men on board the ship. The *Journal* and the *World* published highly sensational accounts of the tragedy as President McKinley worked for weeks to figure out why the ship had exploded.

President McKinley had not been in favor of going to battle, but he declared war on April 25, 1898, beginning the Spanish-American War, which ended about three and a half months later.

Although there are differing theories on why the *USS Maine* exploded and what ignited the Spanish-American War, some historians believe

who were occupying their island country. The Spaniards retaliated against the Cubans by imprisoning a large segment of the Cuban population in concentration camps called *reconcentrados* that provided little food, water, or medical care. This resulted in the starvation and death of hundreds of thousands of Cubans—and angered Americans.

Both Hearst and Pulitzer saw Cuba's struggles for independence as highly engaging news and a way to sell newspapers and potentially help Cubans. Hearst was especially zealous about cov-

sensational newspaper headlines helped fan the flames of the conflict and sway American views in favor of military intervention. According to George H. Douglas, author of *The Golden Age of the Newspaper*, "It has become commonplace to say that the war was as much the product of the jingoism and journalistic saber-rattling of *The Journal* and *The World* as it was of strained relations between Spain and the United States." Jingoism is the act of righteous patriotism toward another country with the intention of aggression or war.

The sensational yellow journalism style lasted until the early 1900s and was eventually replaced with more objective, ethical, and fact-based writing.

THE MIGHTY MUCKRAKERS

"The pen is mightier than the sword."

—Edward Bulwer-Lytton

Muckraker is a term that sounds important yet unpleasant at the same time. The muckrakers were investigative journalists who worked hard to uncover truth and expose corruption and abuse at the turn of the century in the United States. With their keen reporting skills, attention to detail, and fervent words, they would rake up the muck of society, so to speak, to shed light on what was going wrong socially, politically, and economically. These journalists typically wrote for magazines such as *McClure's Magazine*, *Collier's Weekly*, *Munsey's Magazine*, *Scribner's Magazine*, and the *American Magazine*, and they often published books as Nellie Bly did.

Muckrakers were dedicated and relentless journalists who weren't afraid to crusade against societal problems such as child labor, corrupt business, crime, dangerous patent medicines, fraudulent advertising, poor prison conditions, poverty, racial prejudice, shady politics, unethical food production, and unfair employment. They weren't hesitant to cite people's names in their stories. And compared to more sensational styles of journalism, their writing was serious, highly detailed, and factual. Readers were often outraged to learn about what was happening.

The work of these writers inspired social reform. It helped break up large monopolies such as the Standard Oil Company and pass laws such as the Pure Food and Drug Act of 1906 and the Meat Inspection Act of 1906. The muckraking era in America lasted from about 1900 to 1912. It overlapped the Progressive Era, which was a time of social activism and political reform in the United States that lasted from the 1890s until the 1920s.

Theodore Roosevelt, the 26th president of the United States from 1901 until 1908, is

Theodore Roosevelt coined the term *muckraker*. Library of Congress LC-USZC2-6209

CONDUCT AN INTERVIEW

NELLIE WASN'T A TRAINED JOURNALIST, but she excelled at reporting because she was a good interviewer. Journalists need to be skilled at conducting interviews by asking questions and recording what is said. It takes curiosity, practice, and patience.

You'll Need
* Pencil or pen
* Paper or reporter's notebook
* Computer and printer (optional)

1. Choose someone to interview, such as a teacher, parent, grandparent, or coach, and ask that person if he or she is willing to be interviewed. If your interviewee agrees, set up a time and place to meet with the person face to face.

2. Do your research. At the library or online, find out as much about the person ahead of time as possible. You can sometimes research information by talking with others.

3. Write down a list of no more than three to five questions.

4. Meet with the person and ask the questions from your list. It's OK to ask your interviewee to speak slowly. When your interviewee answers a question, take careful notes and write down exactly what he or she says.

5. After the interview is over, thank your interviewee for participating.

6. On a new sheet of paper, write every question you asked followed by the interviewee's answers. Write your initials in capital letters before every question you asked, followed by the interviewee's initials in capitals before each answer.

7. Share your interview with your interviewee and talk about it. How did it go? What did you learn? What did you like or not like about interviewing someone?

credited with coining the term *muckraker* during an April 14, 1906, speech titled "The Man with the Muck-Rake." In his speech, which was a special dedication for the new House of Representatives office building in Washington, DC, Roosevelt voiced his impassioned concerns about journalism. He talked at length about how writers, reporters, and publishers serve an indispensable purpose for the well-being of society but too often expose political scandals and corruption in what he believed was an excessive, unfair, and one-sided way. In short, he didn't like all the dirt digging and mudslinging he saw in the press.

To make his point, Roosevelt referred to a Christian-based allegorical novel titled *The Pilgrim's Progress* written in 1678 by author John Bunyan. In the book, Bunyan describes the man with a muckrake as someone who is always looking down at the ground and never up, and focused solely on raking up the filth of the world and seeing the worst aspects of life. In his speech, Roosevelt said, "Now, it is very necessary that we should not flinch from seeing what is vile and debasing. There is filth on the floor, and it must be scraped up with the muck-rake; and there are times and places where this service is the most needed of all the services that can be performed." But he added that someone whose only focus is on the wrongs of the world becomes "one of the most potent forces for evil."

Roosevelt also asked for truth in reporting without lurid sensationalism and said, "There should be relentless exposure of and attack upon every evil man whether politician or businessman, every evil practice, whether in politics, in business, or in social life. I hail as a benefactor every writer or speaker, every man who, on the platform, or in book, magazine, or newspaper, with merciless severity makes such attack, provided always that he in his turn remembers that the attack is of use only if it is absolutely truthful."

For investigative journalism, muckraking has played an important role in the past as well as the present, and its impact has often brought change and improvements to our world.

Although Roosevelt's use of the term *muckraker* was derogatory, many journalists such as Jacob Riis, Ida Tarbell, Ida B. Wells, and Upton Sinclair considered the term a badge of honor. You'll meet them in the following chapters.

The Art and Science of Investigative Reporting

WHETHER FOR print, broadcast, or the Web, different forms of journalism offer readers and viewers different ways to access information. Although all reporting involves investigation through inquiry and research, investigative journalism is a specific style of reporting designed to ferret out facts and expose the truth.

Investigative journalists work hard to report on what's not right in the world. They often tackle one specific story and work on it at length to present helpful and accurate information. Like sleuths, these reporters interview people, investigate places, and seek out important records that will help bring forth facts and insight to tell a story.

These journalists often write about specific topics such as crime, fraud, greed, unfair business practices, cruelty to people or animals, wrongful convictions, poor living situations, discrimination, or the lack of safety. Story ideas arise from basic questions and observations. *How could that be? Why did that happen? That doesn't look right. That doesn't seem ethical. Is that fair? Whom does that harm?*

Author's collection

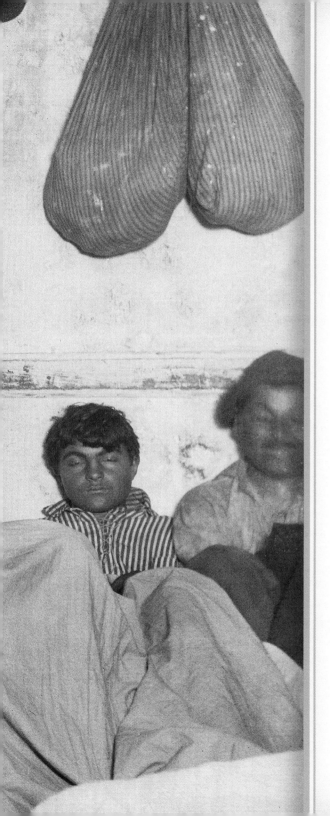

JACOB RIIS

"The half that was on top cared little for the struggles, and less for the fate of those who were underneath, so long as it was able to hold them there and keep its own seat."

—JACOB RIIS

As a young man of 21, Jacob Riis (1849–1914) emigrated from Denmark to America in 1870. It was the same year six-year-old Pink Cochran (aka Nellie Bly) lost her beloved father. Although Jacob and Nellie were 15 years apart in age and miles away from one another at this time, they were both feeling the pangs of loss and separation. Later in their lives they both worked as reporters at various publications in New York City.

Jacob, a gifted writer who used a camera to shed light on the ravages of poverty, became one of the earliest muckrakers and social reformers in America. His life illustrates a remarkable story of transformation: Jacob went

Jacob Riis. Library of Congress LC-USZ62-47078

from being a homeless and penniless immigrant to becoming a close friend of President Theodore Roosevelt and helping improve Americans' lives. Jacob wrote more than a dozen books during his career as a journalist. His acclaimed book *How the Other Half Lives: Studies Among the Tenements of New York*, was published in 1890 and depicts poverty, child labor, and slum conditions, which many families faced in New York City's Lower East Side during the late 1800s. His best-selling autobiography, *The Making of an American*, was published in 1901 and is a compelling account of the American dream.

AN ANCIENT TOWN CALLED RIBE

Jacob Riis was born on May 3, 1849, in the picturesque coastal town of Ribe, Denmark. Located on the North Sea, just south of Sweden and Norway, Ribe is the oldest town in Denmark. It was a beautiful place to grow up. Jacob loved to be outdoors in a world of windmills, cobblestone roads lit by whale-oil lanterns, boats, waterways, bridges, tulip-filled fields, and reed-strewn marshes. It was common to see swans, geese, and storks gliding across waterways or nesting atop buildings. And when his town flooded, as it occasionally did, Jacob and his friends enjoyed fishing for trout or grayling on the newly formed street streams.

Jacob grew up in a large family with 12 brothers, a sister named Sophie, and a cousin named Emma whom the family adopted when her mother died. Six of Jacob's brothers died of tuberculosis, and one drowned. Jacob's parents were devout and highly respected individuals in their small Ribe community. Jacob's mother showed him early examples of charity toward others, and his father taught English and Latin at the local school and wrote editorials for the town paper.

Headstrong Jacob didn't like school and was sometimes a troublemaker; a schoolmarm once threatened to snip his ear with scissors as a punishment. But at home, Jacob liked to read in both Danish and English, and his knowledge of the world grew through journals and books. Every week Charles Dickens's journal, *All the Year Round*, would show up at his house with "stories ever so much more alluring than the tedious grammar." Jacob also liked to delve into historical novels such as *The Last of the Mohicans* by American novelist James Fenimore Cooper and the fairy tales of Danish author Hans Christian Andersen.

FIRST LOVE

Although Jacob's father hoped his son would become a professional writer or educator one day, Jacob traveled to Copenhagen when he was 15 to learn the craft of carpentry. In Copenhagen,

Jacob was homesick for a young girl he adored named Elisabeth Nielsen Giørtz. When Jacob returned to Ribe four years later, he immediately proposed marriage to Elisabeth, but she declined. Heartbroken, Jacob wrote in his autobiography, "I kissed her hands and went out, my eyes brimming over with tears, feeling that there was nothing in all the wide world for me any more, and that the farther I went from her the better. So it was settled that I should go to America."

Before Jacob moved away, Elisabeth's mother gave him a curl of her daughter's blond hair in a gold locket and a photo of her. "I lived on that picture and that curl six long years," Jacob said.

A NEW LIFE IN AMERICA

"I had a pair of strong hands, and stubbornness enough to do for two; also a strong belief that in a free country, free from the dominion of custom, of caste, as well as of men, things would somehow come right in the end..."

—Jacob Riis

From the mid-1800s to the early 1900s, millions of immigrants traveled to America in search of a better, happier life with more political and religious freedom. Immigrants came from all parts of the world and especially from northern and western Europe. Jacob Riis was one such immigrant. He left Ribe when he was 21 years old, with a few dollars in his pocket and big dreams for his future.

On board the *Iowa* steamship that set sail from Glasgow, Scotland, Jacob traveled steerage class, which was the least expensive way to travel across the Atlantic to America. But it meant hunkering down with hundreds of other people in cramped, dark, and foul-smelling quarters below the ship's decks.

After two and a half weeks on the steamer, Jacob arrived at the immigration port of Castle Garden in New York City. He must have felt inspired to land at the regal-sounding port, which was the destination for millions of immigrants arriving in America before Ellis Island opened in 1892. Jacob described landing in America: "It was a beautiful spring morning, and as I looked over the rail at the miles of straight streets, the green heights of Brooklyn, and the stir of ferryboats and pleasure craft on the river, my hopes rose high that somewhere in this teeming hive there would be a place for me." Yes, there would be a place for Jacob, but he would not find it for years.

Upon arriving in New York City, Jacob promptly spent half his money to buy a pistol, which he wore in a holster, cowboy-style, as he strode about the streets of New York trying to look tough. A friendly policeman, seeing Jacob's naiveté, quickly suggested he leave the gun at home, which Jacob did thereafter.

Jacob needed to find work. His first job took him to Brady's Bend Iron Works, near Pittsburgh, Pennsylvania, where he was hired to build huts for coal miners. Hoping to increase his wages, Jacob tried his hand at coal mining. After being nearly crushed by a falling boulder and momentarily trapped in a pitch-black mine shaft, he quickly gave up prospecting.

Finding work, food, and a place to sleep in America was not as easy as Jacob had imagined. After only one month in his new country, he wanted to go home. He raced from Pennsylvania back to New York with just one cent in his pocket. Unfortunately, he didn't have the means or money to return to Denmark.

One night, feeling discouraged and lost, he slept in a milk wagon. "I walked till the stars in the east began to pale, and then climbed into a wagon that stood at the curb to sleep. I did not notice that it was a milk-wagon. The sun had not risen yet when the driver came, unceremoniously dragged me out by the feet, and dumped me into the gutter."

PENNILESS AND HUNGRY

NOT ABLE to find a way home, Jacob "joined the great army of tramps," looking for something, anything, to eat. Traveling up and down the railroad tracks in search of odd jobs, Jacob stopped in rural areas to work as a farmhand.

He slept in fields, barns, or even graveyards at night, wondering if he'd ever see his mom, dad, or beloved Elisabeth again.

As days grew long and difficult, Jacob had an overpowering sense of loss and desperation. His only companion was a sweet dog he'd found wandering the streets. One rainy night, Jacob stayed at the dilapidated Church Street police station where his bed was a wooden plank with no blanket. The next morning, his gold locket with Elisabeth's hair was gone . . . and his dog was killed. Jacob became hysterical with grief. "Raving like a madman, I stormed the police station with paving-stones from the gutter."

Angry and dejected, Jacob left the police station that day. But he didn't give up. Over the following months, he scavenged for food and found odd jobs as a bricklayer, carpenter, caretaker, and salesman. He managed to survive. Although painful, this time in his life was an important stepping-stone. He learned what it felt like to be poor, hungry, homeless, and mistreated. These experiences paved the way for his future work as a muckraker fighting for social reform.

A SMART IDEA

JACOB EVENTUALLY saved enough money to attend school and learn telegraphy, which was an up-and-coming technology for transmitting messages. The telegraphy school principal was impressed with Jacob and helped him land a reporting job in 1873 at the *New York News Association,* located in New York's Newspaper Row. This entry-level newspaper job set Jacob on a writing path that resulted in lifelong work as a reporter, photographer, lecturer, and author. Over the years, Jacob worked at various papers in New York, including the *South Brooklyn News* (1874), the *New York Tribune* (1877–1888), and the *New York Evening Sun* (1888–1899).

In 1876, five years after arriving in America and feeling more confident about his career, Jacob wrote to Elisabeth and once again asked her to marry him. This time, she accepted. Jacob traveled to Denmark to be married and returned with his true love, whom he affectionately called Lammet (the Danish word for *lamb*). The couple raised five children and were happily married for 25 years.

In 1877, one year after marrying Elisabeth, Jacob's life took a surprisingly good turn. While frantically rushing back to the *Tribune* offices to meet a deadline, he accidentally knocked over his editor, who landed in a snowdrift. "Is that the way you treat your city editor, Riis?" his boss growled. Devastated, Jacob was sure he'd be fired. Instead, the next day Jacob was promoted to be a police reporter at the Mulberry Street police headquarters. "You can run there all you want to, and you will want to all you can," his boss said.

Jacob's new job on the police beat took him straight into the notorious slums of New York City's densely populated Lower East Side. He would head out in the middle of the night to the slum neighborhoods of Five Points and Mulberry Bend to cover everything from murders and fires to suicides and robberies. It was a world of gangs, poverty, disease, crime, gambling, and despair. At times Jacob found himself in the middle of deadly saloon brawls.

PHOTOGRAPHS FOR REFORM

As a police reporter, Jacob regularly witnessed the dilapidated living conditions in the New York City slums. He saw children and adults huddled together in unsanitary rooms with poor ventilation, dim light, and lack of proper plumbing. He saw parents sleeping on floors and children sleeping in cardboard boxes. He knew that many individuals, especially children, died in the tenement houses owned by slumlords who ignored unhealthy conditions yet charged high rents. Jacob began to focus on the slums and the efforts being made to improve them. He realized photographs could show readers the horrific conditions he had seen in the different tenement neighborhoods.

Jacob bought a simple wooden box camera and used a newly invented flash powder technique that could ignite and light up completely dark areas. This enabled him to take photographs in dark tenement rooms. Although flash powder was extremely dangerous and sometimes set fires, it was a godsend for Jacob. On many nights in 1888, Jacob ventured into tenement apartments, set up his photography equipment, and exposed a world many people knew nothing about.

Jacob exhibited the tenement photographs in an entertaining and educational lecture series called *The Other Half: How It Lives and Dies in New York*. A natural showman, Jacob enjoyed lecturing. He presented the photos as a slum tour guide, leading audiences from one squalid neighborhood to the next. Audiences were riveted by the series.

Newspapers, magazines, and publishers took notice of Jacob's work. In December 1889, images of his tenement photos were featured in an article he wrote for *Scribner's Magazine*. The photos were then featured in Jacob's groundbreaking book, *How the Other Half Lives: Studies Among the Tenements of New York*, published by Charles

Jacob photographed families living in New York City tenements.

Jacob A. Riis/Museum of the City of New York

Jacob Riis used a wooden box camera like this one, which is an Antique Oak Detective Camera from the early 1890s. Courtesy Rob Niederman

"MY TOWN" PHOTO ESSAY

JACOB RIIS USED A CAMERA to capture important images of New York City's Lower East Side. In many ways, Jacob's images revealed more than words could ever say. Journalists often use cameras to add photographic images to their written words.

A photo essay tells a story with images and is often displayed for others to see. Create a trifold photo essay that visually describes where you live.

You'll Need

* Camera
* 5–10 photographs taken around your town
* Computer and printer (optional)
* Scissors
* 3 sheets heavy card stock 8½ by 11 inches (21.6 cm by 28 cm)
* Tape
* Craft glue or glue stick
* Decorative paper (optional)
* Pencil or pen

1. Take five to ten photos around your town of different places, people, animals, or buildings that depict where you live.

2. Print your photos at a photo lab, or print them from your computer and cut them out. A good photo size is 3 by 5 inches (7.6 by 12.7-cm) or 4 by 6 inches (10.2 by 15.2 cm). You can also cut photos to smaller sizes.

3. Make a trifold with the three sheets of card stock. Place them vertically, in a row. Tape these sheets together (front and back), leaving a slight gap between the sheets so you can fold them. Trim excess tape.

4. Glue the photos to your trifold; you can also glue decorative paper behind your photos.

5. Write captions (descriptive words) below each photo and title your essay.

6. Display your photo essay for others to see.

Lewis W. Hine's Images of Child Labor

BORN IN Oshkosh, Wisconsin, in 1874, Lewis Wickes Hine studied education in college and taught school at the Ethical Culture School in New York City in the early 1900s. Intrigued by photography, Lewis encouraged his students to use the camera as a documentary tool. He took his students on outings throughout the city to photograph the tenement houses and the many immigrants arriving at Ellis Island.

Like Jacob Riis, Lewis photographed the people and poverty he observed in America during the turn of the century. He didn't like how children were often exploited as workers, and his camera became a powerful tool to bring about change.

In 1907, Congress chartered the National Child Labor Committee (NCLC) to help poor, uneducated children who were used as child laborers. The NCLC hired Lewis as a staff investigator to photograph children working in places such as glass factories, cotton mills, coal mines, and canneries. He took along a small notebook to interview the children in his photos and jot down their names and information about their lives.

From New York to Pennsylvania, Tennessee, Alabama, and beyond, Lewis's photographs helped show Americans firsthand the serious issues of child labor, which brought about much needed social reform.

A 12-year-old girl makes money sewing lace collars. Library of Congress LC-DIG-nclc-04130

Scribner's Sons. Like his lecture series' slum tour, *How the Other Half Lives* presented individual chapters about the different ethnic neighborhoods Jacob photographed. Years later, the book was criticized for Jacob's stereotypic and derogatory descriptions of ethnic and racial groups, which would not be acceptable today. But in 1890, the book became a bestseller, raised public awareness of slum conditions, and led to reform.

Theodore Roosevelt, who served as president for the New York Board of Police Commissioners from 1895 to 1897, read *How the Other Half Lives* and offered to help. He and Jacob walked the streets of the slums at night to investigate the tenements firsthand. In time, Roosevelt closed down the deplorable police station lodges and helped pass legislation to demolish the worst tenement houses and build new parks and public schools in poor neighborhoods.

Jacob was a key figure in helping turn the impoverished Mulberry Bend area into a grassy park in 1897. He also devoted his energies to helping community charity houses (such as the King's Daughters Settlement House) that provided child care, health care, recreation, and instruction for children and parents. In 1901 the King's Daughters Settlement House was renamed the Jacob A. Riis Neighborhood Settlement House. Today, it continues to provide services for New York's underserved children and parents.

✳

DESIGN HISTORIC GREETING CARDS

YOU CAN FIND HUNDREDS of Lewis W. Hine's photographs online in the Prints and Photographs Division of the Library of Congress in Washington, DC. These historic photographs can be used to make unique turn-of-the-century greeting cards.

You'll Need

* Card stock 8½ by 11 inches (21.6 by 28 cm)
* Pencil or pen
* Ruler
* Scissors
* Bone folder (a small crafting tool that makes a sharp crease), available at art supply stores
* Computer and printer with Microsoft Word
* Printer paper 8½ by 11 inches (21.6 by 28 cm)
* Craft glue or glue stick

1. On the card stock, use a ruler and pencil to measure and draw a rectangular card, 6½ inches (16.5 cm) wide by 10 inches (25 cm) tall. Cut out the card and erase the pencil lines.

2. Use the ruler again to find the middle of the card at 5 inches (12.7 cm), and draw a faint horizontal pencil line across the card.

3. With the ruler and bone folder, crease the middle of the card so it's easier to fold. To do this, place the ruler at the middle line and hold it down firmly. Then, drag a bone folder along the ruler about 10 times to form a crease. When your crease is visible, fold the card over (making sure to match the ends of the card first), and press the crease to flatten the card.

4. Go online to www.loc.gov/pictures/ to find Lewis W. Hine photos. When you've opened this link, type *LOT 7481* in the search bar and click *GO*. This will take you to more than 250 Lewis Hine photos (view them by clicking the Gallery option).

5. Click on a photo you like, which will open a larger image.

6. Place your cursor over the photo you like; holding down the cursor, drag the photo to your computer desktop, where it will appear as a JPEG file. You can now drag the photo into a blank document page, such as a page in a Word document, and save it.

7. Print the image.

8. Your photo will need to be smaller. Use the ruler and pencil to measure and draw a rectangle around the photo that is approximately 4 by 6 inches (10.2 by 15.2 cm) in size. Cut out the photo.

9. Glue the photo to the face of the card. Gently erase any pencil lines.

10. Write a message inside your card.

Ida Tarbell.

The Ida M. Tarbell Collection,
Pelletier Library, Allegheny College

IDA TARBELL

"Imagination is the only key to the future.
Without it none exists—with it all things are possible."

—IDA TARBELL

Wealthy oil tycoon John D. Rockefeller always called her "Miss Tar Barrel." But that didn't stop feisty journalist Ida Tarbell (1857–1944) from standing up to Mr. Rockefeller and his multimillion-dollar oil monopoly with her revolutionary book, *The History of the Standard Oil Company*.

Ida Minerva Tarbell was a pioneer in real life as well as in journalism and social reform. She was born in a rustic log cabin in northwestern Pennsylvania two years before the birth of the oil industry, four years before the start of the Civil War, and seven years before Nellie Bly was born. Ida was one of the first women to graduate from Allegheny College in Pennsylvania and was a leading progressive journalist and muckraker of her time.

Like fellow journalist Nellie Bly, Ida's writing career blossomed in New York City. Both Ida and Nellie moved from their home state of Pennsylvania to work in New York where more reporting jobs were slowly opening up for women. They both faced the challenges of being a woman and working in the field of journalism in the late 1800s and early 1900s.

In addition to publishing *The History of the Standard Oil Company*, Ida penned articles and books about iconic figures, including Napoleon Bonaparte and Abraham Lincoln. Ida became cofounder and coeditor of the *American Magazine* in 1906 and wrote her autobiography, *All in the Day's Work*, when she was 80 years old.

A PENNSYLVANIA PIONEER

IDA WAS born in Hatch Hollow, Pennsylvania, on November 5, 1857. Her father, Franklin Tarbell, was miles away in Iowa searching for a new home for his family when Esther Tarbell gave birth to their first child. Esther named the baby girl Ida Minerva, which stood for hardworking and wise. But without enough money to purchase land in Iowa, Franklin returned to Hatch Hollow when his daughter was a year and a half old. When Ida first laid eyes on the strange man, she clung to her mother and cried out, "Go away, bad man," she recalled in her autobiography. But Ida came to love her father and later described him as a friendly, honest, and hardworking man.

Ida grew up with a younger brother, Will, a younger sister, Sarah, and a baby brother, Frankie, who died of scarlet fever. Her father worked in carpentry as a joiner, specializing in building wooden structures such as doors, window frames, and eventually, oil tanks.

LIQUID GOLD

FRANK TARBELL still had dreams to move his family to the wide-open, flower-filled spaces of Iowa. But everything changed in 1859 as an oil rush began near Titusville, Pennsylvania, located about 40 miles from Hatch Hollow.

For many years, residents of Oil Creek Valley near Titusville had noticed petroleum (crude oil) naturally seeping up on the land or sitting atop the surface water of nearby Oil Creek. This oil was sometimes skimmed up and used sparingly in products such as medicinal ointments or as a lubricant for machinery. Some people drank it as a cure-all. In time, inventors figured out how to refine crude oil and convert it to kerosene so it could be used as fuel to light lamps. Previously, whale oil had been used as lamp fuel, but it was expensive and difficult to obtain. Once people realized crude oil could be used as a new energy source for lighting, they wanted at it.

Edwin Drake, a railroad worker from Connecticut, was hired to see if he could find and extract oil near Oil Creek. Drake worked with blacksmith William Smith ("Uncle Billy"), who had experience drilling for salt, a naturally occurring product also mined in Pennsylvania. Drake cleverly positioned an engine house with a derrick directly over a large oil seepage. Salt-drilling equipment boosted with steam power was used to bore down into the earth in search of the "liquid gold." It was a slow process, but Uncle Billy kept at it, drilling deeper and deeper into the bedrock below. His hard work almost seemed futile. People started calling Edwin "Crazy Drake." But when Uncle Billy drilled to 69 feet in the earth, something happened. On the morning of August 27, 1859, a dark green substance floated up and around the drill head. It didn't spout like an oil gusher, but sure enough, it was oil. That day, Drake and Uncle Billy hand pumped the oil and poured it into washtubs used as temporary holding tanks. The oil rose upward, and gallon after gallon was poured into whiskey barrels. It was a crucial breakthrough and the beginning of the US petroleum industry. News of Drake's discovery spread, and thousands were drawn to the area to make their fortunes.

Frank Tarbell realized he could use his carpentry skills to build large wooden tanks to hold the oil pouring out of the Pennsylvania earth.

Suddenly, he had a new business venture, and moving to Iowa could wait.

In a horse-pulled buggy, Frank drove his family over the Allegheny foothills to a new home and workshop in Rouseville, near Edwin Drake's original well. Their new abode looked like a simple wooden shanty, and three-year-old Ida wasn't thrilled. "My first reaction to my new surroundings was one of acute dislike," she later recalled. Ida missed her old log cabin and playing outdoors

Ida grew up surrounded by oil wells.
Library of Congress LC-USZ62-63520

CRAFT AN OIL GUSHER DIORAMA

AS A YOUNG GIRL, Ida lived on the edge of an active oil field. Oil wells called gushers would shoot oil into the air that would shower down and coat the nearby trees, shrubs, grass, and flowers. To escape from this "greasy" world, Ida liked to hike to the nearby hillside where the forest was alive and pristine.

It's hard to imagine living in an oil town like Ida's, but you can create a small model of one.

Adult supervision required

You'll Need

* Natural items such as branches, twigs, flowers, sand, and rocks
* Styrofoam base [a circular green floral foam disc about 6 inches (15.2 cm) across works well]
* Camera (optional)
* 2 tablespoons of black acrylic paint
* ¼ cup water
* Small, 5-inch-tall (13 cm) plastic spray bottle
* Recycled newspaper pages

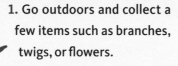

1. Go outdoors and collect a few items such as branches, twigs, or flowers.

2. Stick these items securely into the Styrofoam base to create a natural, forest-like setting. You can also add rocks and sand. Take a photo of your project now if you like.

3. Next, mix the black paint with the water in the spray bottle and shake it.

4. Move your diorama outdoors or to an area such as a garage or workshop. Place the diorama on top of about four newspaper pages that are spread out, and cover and protect nearby walls and objects. You don't want the paint to coat anything but your diorama.

5. Carefully spritz the diorama with the paint and see how it coats your landscape. Take a photo of your project now.

6. Think about it. How did your diorama look before it was drenched with paint? How does it look now? What would it have been like to live where Ida did?

with the many ducks, turkeys, chickens, lambs, colts, calves, kittens, and puppies around her home. Rouseville was fraught with peril. A creek near the shanty rushed wildly, large oil pits were everywhere, and wooden oil derricks were not to be climbed. Mortified by this wild, inky new world, young Ida decided to walk back to Hatch Hollow by herself. But when the journey quickly proved too difficult, she returned to her mother, who was glad to have her home. Ida said, "Respect for my mother [and] her wisdom in dealing with hard situations, was born then."

Frank's business grew with the booming oil industry. The Oil Creek region was a world of "fountain wells, gushers and spouters" and people wanting to get rich quick. Where oil gushed out of the earth, the nearby trees, shrubs, and grass were coated with the blackish substance and died. In her autobiography, Ida wrote, "No industry of man in its early days has ever been more destructive of beauty, order, decency, than the production of petroleum."

Oil could be highly volatile, and people lost their lives in explosions and fires. In one horrific disaster during Ida's youth, a light ignited gas flowing from a well and caused a huge explosion. Nineteen men burned to death. Ida's mother took care of one man who had been severely burned and saved his life.

Ida watched the oil industry grow, "producing some thirty-three million barrels of crude oil," over the 10 years since the family had moved to Rouseville. In addition to Frank's tank business, the oil industry kept people busy producing, transporting, refining, marketing, and exporting oil. But there were big changes ahead.

COLLEGE AND A CAREER

IN 1870, when 21-year-old Jacob Riis was traveling to America for the first time, Ida was 13 and moving with her family from Rouseville to Titusville, a larger, more established community about 10 miles away. Frank built the family an attractive home, and Ida, Will, and Sarah were enrolled in public schools. At first Ida didn't like the large, crowded classrooms in Titusville and would ditch school. But she gradually became an excellent student and graduated at the top of her class. School opened her eyes to a love of science, and she became enamored with looking at leaves, rocks, and flowers under a microscope. Her ambitions as a teen were unusual and forward thinking for her day and age. Ida wanted to go to college and achieve financial independence through a career. Marriage was not on her to-do list.

When Ida was 19, she became a freshman at Allegheny College in Meadville, Pennsylvania, which was about 30 miles from her home. She was the only woman in a class of 40 boys; four years later, in 1880, Ida graduated with a major in biology. Although Ida wanted to work as a biologist, there were few job openings for women in science. Ida did find work as a teacher at the Poland Union Seminary in Poland, Ohio, and worked there, somewhat unhappily, for two years.

Ida's next job was as an assistant editor at *The Chautauquan*, a magazine-format teaching guide published by the Chautauqua Institution in Meadville. It was a thrilling time for Ida. She gained important editing and writing skills and quickly moved up as an editor. She also started to travel to conduct research, which took her to places such as the Washington, DC, patent office for an article about women's inventions.

TO PARIS AND BEYOND

As IDA's writing career flourished, she was eager to visit new cities, see the world, and take on bigger writing assignments. She wanted freedom to expand her life and work and decided to move to Paris to write a biography about Madame Marie-Jeanne Roland, who was a political activist during the French Revolution. Before being beheaded, Madame Roland uttered her legendary words, "O Liberty! Liberty! how many crimes are committed in thy name."

Theodore Flood, Ida's editor at *The Chautauquan*, tried to dissuade Ida from going abroad, saying, "You're not a writer. You'll starve!"

PERFECT PARFAIT FOR A SCRIBE

WHEN IDA WAS LIVING and writing in Paris, she didn't have a lot of money for extravagant meals. But if she did splurge for a treat, she may have had a delicious dessert called a *parfait* (par-FAY), which means "perfect" in French. You might enjoy making a yogurt and fruit parfait.

You'll Need

* ¾ cup raspberries
* ¾ cup blueberries
* Strainer
* Small bowls
* Spoon
* 6 oz. vanilla yogurt (about ¾ cup)
* Medium-size glass
* ¼ cup granola

1. Rinse the raspberries and blueberries separately in a strainer, and drain them.

2. Place the fruit in separate bowls.

3. Spoon about two tablespoons of yogurt in the bottom of your glass.

4. Add a few blueberries on top of the yogurt.

5. Spoon in another layer of yogurt.

6. Add a layer of raspberries.

7. Repeat the yogurt and fruit layers to the top of the glass.

8. Top with the granola.

Thankfully, Ida knew better and didn't take his so-called advice. Once in Paris, Ida rented an apartment in the more inexpensive, bohemian Latin Quarter, where she lived for three years, from 1891 to 1894. She worked on her book about Madame Roland and wrote articles for various US newspapers and magazines. Her byline became more prominent in publications such as the *Pittsburgh Dispatch* (where Nellie Bly got her start as a writer) as well as the *Chicago Tribune*, *Cincinnati Times-Star*, and *Scribner's Magazine*. Although making money was always a challenge, Ida was an American journalist in Paris, and her life was fascinating. She met many innovative thinkers, writers, artists, and politicians in Paris and learned about the world beyond her hometown.

In 1892 when Ida was 35, her life took an auspicious turn when she met newspaperman Samuel McClure in Paris. McClure founded the McClure Syndicate, America's first newspaper syndicate. A newspaper syndicate, such as King Features or Tribune Media Services today, sells materials such as columns, feature stories, and comics for publication in a number of newspapers or magazines simultaneously.

McClure commissioned Ida to write newspaper articles about French women writers and the French chemist Louis Pasteur, known for the pasteurization of milk. In 1893, Ida also published her essay, "Madame Roland," in *Scribner's*

Magazine; she then published her book, *Madame Roland: A Biographical Study*, with publisher Charles Scribner's Sons a few years later.

Ida was working hard and writing like crazy, but after three years in Paris she missed her family and headed home to Titusville. It wasn't long before Ida was on her way again—this time to New York City to work for Samuel McClure, who had just started the dynamic new monthly magazine called *McClure's Magazine*. McClure hired Ida fulltime in 1894, and her first assignments included writing biographical sketches of Napoleon Bonaparte and Abraham Lincoln. Her impressive series about these two famous leaders nearly doubled the circulation of *McClure's* and earned Ida national recognition.

STANDING UP TO STANDARD

As the staff at *McClure's* grew, the magazine started to publish more investigative stories about issues such as municipal corruption and business monopolies (also known as trusts), which readers were eager to know about. In her autobiography, Ida wrote, "The deluge of monopolistic trusts, which had followed the close of the Spanish-American War and the 'return of prosperity' was disturbing and confusing people."

Ida proposed a series of articles about the biggest monopoly of the time, John D. Rockefeller's Standard Oil trust, which had blown into the Oil Creek region where Ida grew up and put many smaller oil companies out of business. Ida knew about Standard Oil firsthand; her father's small oil tank business had suffered terribly from it. The Standard Oil Company took over the petroleum market by buying up small oil refineries and monopolizing the railway system to transport crude oil and kerosene.

THE HISTORY OF
THE STANDARD OIL COMPANY

BY

IDA M. TARBELL

AUTHOR OF
THE LIFE OF ABRAHAM LINCOLN, THE LIFE OF NAPOLEON BONAPARTE, AND MADAME ROLAND: A BIOGRAPHICAL STUDY

ILLUSTRATED WITH PORTRAITS PICTURES AND DIAGRAMS

VOLUME ONE

NEW YORK
McCLURE, PHILLIPS & CO.
MCMV

Ida Tarbell's book is an exposé of the Standard Oil Company.

McClure's Magazine

ONE OF the most popular muckraking publications of the early 1900s was *McClure's Magazine*, published from 1893 to 1929. Cofounded by publisher Samuel Sidney McClure, who immigrated to America from Ireland in 1866 when he was nine years old, the magazine sold for the low cost of 10 cents and offered readers well-written articles and many illustrations. The magazine first featured fiction writing, including articles by American author Mark Twain and English novelist Rudyard Kipling.

In the early 1900s, McClure leaned toward nonfiction and included more investigative reporting in his magazine. He began to hire investigative journalists. The January 1903 edition of *McClure's* stands out as a milestone in journalism history. It featured three in-depth investigative articles: Ida Tarbell's second article about the history of the Standard Oil Company, writer Lincoln Steffens's article about city corruption titled "The Shame of Minneapolis," and writer Ray Stannard Baker's article about non-striking coal miners titled "The Right to Work."

When the *McClure's* readership began to wane, Tarbell, Steffens, and Baker left the magazine in 1906 and founded their own publication called the *American Magazine*, which continued to focus on social reform issues.

McClure's Magazine featured muckraking journalists. Wikimedia Commons

Ida worked for many years researching and writing her seminal (groundbreaking) pieces on Standard Oil to expose the unscrupulous business practices the company used that severely hurt competition in the oil industry. Her articles were published in 19 installments in *McClure's Magazine* from 1902 to 1904 and then compiled into the book, *The History of the Standard Oil Company*, published in 1904 by McClure, Phillips & Company. Ida's eye-opening book led to an investigation by the federal government and resulted in a 1911 US Supreme Court decision to break up the large Standard Oil monopoly into 34 separate companies.

HER ACTIONS AND WORDS LIVE ON

AFTER IDA'S father died in 1905, she moved to a large farm in Connecticut and helped cofound and coedit the *American Magazine* with fellow journalists Ray Stannard Baker, Lincoln Steffens, and John Sanborn Phillips. Ida wrote extensively for the new magazine and often focused on articles about unfair practices in American corporations and business.

Over the following decades Ida penned numerous books, including eight books about Abraham Lincoln and two books about women titled *The Ways of Women* (1915) and *The Business of Being a Woman* (1921). Her books about women surprised readers because, although she advocated for safe and fair work conditions for working women, she strongly believed women's most important role was in the home. This was in part because Ida grew up during a time when most women married and worked at home raising their children. If a woman worked outside the home, typical careers were in teaching or nursing.

But Ida Tarbell was different and sought a career as a journalist, working side by side with men in a male-dominated field. Although she didn't like being called a muckraker, Ida was a successful writer and supported herself independently. It wasn't easy, and she was sometimes criticized for stepping outside traditional norms, which may have given her reservations about women's roles. Although Ida supported working women's rights, she opposed women's right to vote and wrote in her autobiography, "Feeling as I did, I could not fight for suffrage, although I did not fight against it."

Nonetheless, Ida Tarbell was one of our nation's most famous investigative reporters and remains an important role model for journalists today. Her excellent writing, keen investigative skills, and exceptional work speak volumes. In 1922 the *New York Times* named her one of the "twelve greatest American women." When Ida died of pneumonia in 1944, her January 17, 1944, obituary in the *New York Times* said, "Miss Tarbell was the type of woman who by sheer grit and hard work raised herself from mediocrity to prominence, not only in the field of writing but in the domain of social work."

✳

IDA B. WELLS

"The way to right wrongs is to turn the light of truth upon them."

—IDA B. WELLS

Just two years before the birth of Elizabeth Jane Cochran (Nellie Bly), Ida Bell Wells (1862–1931) was born into slavery during the Civil War (1861–1865) at a time of great change for America. She became an acclaimed journalist and early civil rights leader who dedicated her life to social reform and women's rights. Through her voice and the power of her words, Ida shed light on the brutal practice of lynching and fought for important civil rights for African Americans. Her tireless work helped save lives, awaken others to human rights abuses, and initiate change for this country. But it was a painful road to travel.

On January 1, 1863, about six months after Ida was born, President Abraham Lincoln issued the Emancipation Proclamation, which proclaimed freedom for more than three million slaves of the approximately four million slaves living in the United States at the time. After the Civil War ended, the Reconstruction Era (1865–1877) was a complex time of rebuilding the United States that had been so severely divided. The Confederate states reintegrated with the Union, and the Civil Rights Amendments constitutionally guaranteed rights for African Americans. The 13th Amendment abolished slavery in all states, the 14th Amendment prohibited states from depriving any citizen equality under the law, and the 15th Amendment granted voting rights for African American men.

But the difficult issues surrounding slavery didn't disappear overnight. The Civil Rights Amendments were often violated in the South, which created an unjust, segregated, dangerous, and often deadly world for African Americans—a world Wells abhorred.

A prolific writer, Ida B. Wells published three major antilynching works: *Southern Horrors: Lynch Law in All Its Phases* in 1892, *A Red Record* in 1895, and *Mob Rule in New Orleans* in 1900. Ida's autobiography, *A Crusade for Justice: The Autobiography of Ida B. Wells*, was edited and published in 1970 by her daughter, Alfreda M. Duster. Ida's diary, *The Memphis Diary of Ida B. Wells*, which she wrote during her years in Memphis, was edited and published by Miriam DeCosta-Willis in 1995.

In addition to being a writer, Ida was a dedicated activist and organizer. She spoke out fervently against lynching, carrying her message all across America, to Europe, and even to the White House. She challenged segregation, helped found organizations such as the National Association for the Advancement of Colored People (NAACP), and worked for women's right to vote. In 1930 when Ida was 68, she ran unsuccessfully for the Illinois state senate.

A RECONSTRUCTED LIFE

IDA B. Wells was born in Holly Springs, Mississippi, on July 16, 1862, about 15 months after the start of the Civil War. Her parents, Jim and Lizzie Wells, were slaves until their freedom was granted with the issuing of the Emancipation Proclamation. Ida's father was a skilled carpenter and builder, her mother was a cook, and she had three sisters and four brothers; two of her brothers died.

After the Civil War, Ida's parents were committed to helping create a better world in America for African Americans, and they prospered in their personal and political lives. Before Reconstruction, slaves were denied an education and not allowed to attend school or even learn how to read or write. But change was beginning to take root. The Freedmen's Aid Society was founded in 1861 by the American Missionary Association (a Protestant abolitionist group) and, through church-based efforts, helped open many public schools for blacks in the South. Ida's parents were eager for her to get an education. Ida and her siblings attended Rust College (originally called Shaw University), which provided classes from the elementary levels to high school. "Our job was to go to school and learn all we could," Ida said.

Like many African Americans during Reconstruction, Ida's parents took an active role in helping shape educational opportunities for blacks. Young or old, African Americans wanted to learn; it was an essential right of freedom. Ida's father was a trustee of Rust College, and her mother also attended the school to learn to read the Bible. Ida enjoyed school, did well in her courses, and loved to read. She learned about the world when she read the newspaper to her father. "He was interested in politics and I heard the words Ku Klux Klan long before I knew what they meant. I knew dimly that it meant something fearful, by the anxious way my mother walked the floor at night when my father was out to a political meeting."

The Ku Klux Klan was founded in 1865 during Reconstruction. It was sometimes called the

Ida B. Wells.

Hooded Order because members wore sinister-looking white pointed hoods to hide their faces. Acting as a secret vigilante group, the KKK's purpose was control of African Americans, who were gaining new rights and opportunities. Their tactics of nighttime lynchings, cross-burnings, and rallies were outside the law and were meant to terrorize and intimidate, and they also murdered people who supported African Americans.

Although the term *lynching* is most often associated with the criminal act of causing a person's death by hanging, a lynching can also be defined in a broader sense as the criminal act of causing a person's death by mob violence such as a shooting or bodily attack.

SOUTHERN HORRORS.
LYNCH LAW
IN ALL
ITS PHASES

Miss IDA B. WELLS.

Price.   -   Fifteen Cents.

THE NEW YORK AGE PRINT.
1892.

Ida wrote extensively to expose and stop lynching.

YELLOW FEVER

WHEN IDA turned 16 in 1878, her life changed forever. The yellow fever epidemic had hit Memphis, Tennessee, and spread 50 miles south to Holly Springs. Ida was visiting her grandmother's farm when she learned the sad news that both her parents had contracted yellow fever and died. She later learned that her baby brother Stanley had also died. Concerned about what would happen to her orphaned siblings, Ida boarded a freight train to Holly Springs, even though she knew she might also contract the disease and die. As the oldest Wells child and the big sister, Ida stepped up to take care of her younger brothers and sisters. Her childhood was over; Ida needed to make money to provide for her family.

A friend of the Wells family suggested Ida should become a teacher, and she soon found work at a school in rural Mississippi. On Sunday afternoons Ida would ride a stubborn mule named Ginger and travel six miles to her school. She'd stay at the school for the week and then ride the mule back to Holly Springs on Friday for a chore-filled weekend of cooking food and washing clothes for her siblings in preparation for the following week. Although Ida did not enjoy teaching, it had pluses. As Ida taught her students, she also improved her writing skills and became a voracious reader.

At 19, Ida moved to Memphis with her two younger sisters, Annie and Lily, to live with their Aunt Fannie. Her brothers had found work as carpenter apprentices, and Ida's disabled sister, Eugenia, moved to live with a different aunt. In the big, bustling city of Memphis, Ida found work as a schoolteacher with better pay. She also found more social activities and opportunities to meet and date men. It was an exciting time of growth and change; Ida discovered a new urban world that was unlike the rural life she had led.

In Memphis, public transportation by train seemed a lot easier for Ida compared to riding a mule. But it caused her a great deal of anguish. One Saturday in 1883, when Ida was riding the train from Holly Springs to Memphis, a conductor told her to get out of her first-class seat in the plush, safe, ladies car and move to the uncomfortable smoking car. Having paid for a first-class ticket, Ida resisted and bit the back of the conductor's hand. The conductor then enlisted the help of two other men, who dragged

CHOOSE A PEN NAME

ELIZABETH COCHRANE'S PEN NAME was Nellie Bly, and Ida B. Wells' pen name was Iola.

A pen name, sometimes called a pseudonym, or nom de plume in French, is a substitute name for a reporter or author. Pen names were common during the era when Nellie and Ida were reporters. But they're still used today by writers for different reasons, such as wanting to write anonymously or to have a catchy name readers will remember.

Here are a few famous pen names.

Birth Name	Pen Name
Theodor Seuss Geisel	Dr. Seuss
Joanne Rowling	J. K. Rowling
Samuel Clemens	Mark Twain
Charlotte Brontë	Currer Bell

You'll Need
* Pencil or pen
* Writing paper

1. Coming up with a name can be a creative challenge. Naming bands, albums, brands, or books, for example, takes thought and originality. It also takes time.

2. When choosing a pen name, which could also be used as your byline, stay away from other people's names. Think about original names no one else has. You might use the name of something such as an animal, city, or flower. You might link two unique words for a first and last name, or string together letters and numbers like a password. You might use an acronym like TYVM (thank you very much) or B4N (bye for now).

3. Write a list of 5 to 10 different names. Set your list aside for about a week. Go back to your list and see if one of your pen names seems right for you.

her out of her seat. Angered and humiliated, Ida sued the railroad and won. The case was later appealed, and Ida never received the $500 she was awarded, which made her feel utterly discouraged and discriminated against. But this event was a turning point for Ida, igniting her career as a journalist. She took her words beyond the courtroom and into the newspapers, where people could read about how she was treated.

PRINCESS OF THE PRESS

IN MEMPHIS, Ida joined a literary group of teachers who met Friday afternoons in a church to discuss writing, listen to music, and read from the literary journal the *Evening Star.* Ida became editor of the *Evening Star* and was soon asked to write for a Baptist publication called the *Living Way.* Ida chose the pen name of Iola and wrote in a "plain, common-sense way on the things which concerned our people." She found journalism a lot more inspiring than teaching and said, "The correspondence I had built up in newspaper work gave me an outlet through which to express the real 'me' and I enjoyed my work to the utmost."

Newspapers were starting to hire more women as journalists —such as Nellie Bly, who was then landing her first reporting job at the *Pittsburgh Dispatch.* Ida was first paid as a reporter when hired to write for the weekly *American Baptist* newspaper. This job took her to a Washington, DC, press convention where she met and befriended famed abolitionist Frederick Douglass. She began to write for a number of different black newspapers and made a name for herself as "Iola . . . Princess of the Press."

In 1889, when Ida was 27, she became a part owner of the Memphis *Free Speech and Headlight* newspaper and made the career move from teaching to journalism. "Our [*Free Speech*] circulation had increased in less than a year from fifteen hundred to four thousand, and my salary came to within ten dollars of what I had received as [a] teacher."

LYNCHING AT THE CURVE

IN AN area of Memphis known as the Curve (where the streetcar curved around), Ida's good friend Thomas Moss and his business partners, Calvin McDowell and Henry Stewart, opened the People's Grocery Company, a black-owned store located across the street from a white-owned market. Ida wrote in her autobiography, "He [Thomas] owned his little home, and having saved his money he went into the grocery business with the same ambition that a young white man would have had." But hostilities grew between whites and blacks in the Curve. Thomas was advised to protect his store and stationed armed men at the back of People's on a Saturday night on March 9, 1892. Ida added, "The men stationed there had seen several white men stealing through the rear door and fired on them without a moment's pause. Three of these men were wounded, and others fled and gave the alarm."

The next morning the Memphis newspaper covered the story with lurid, sensational headlines of NEGROES SHOOTING WHITE MEN. Many Southern whites became outraged. "Over a hundred colored men were dragged from their homes and put in jail on suspicion." One night a white mob went to the jail and seized Thomas, Calvin, and Henry. They dragged the men out to the country where they were brutally tortured and shot to death. The mob then went to the People's store and robbed and destroyed it.

Ida had been in Natchez, Mississippi, when the lynching took place and was grief stricken to hear the news. The *Free Speech* newspaper wrote about the lynching and advised African Americans to dispose of their property and move away from Memphis for their own safety. For three weeks Ida traveled to Oklahoma to check out and describe the safer conditions there; her articles were posted in *Free Speech*. Many African Americans did leave Memphis and moved west to states such as Arkansas, Oklahoma, and beyond.

Ida considered moving to Oklahoma but headed east to New York to meet with T. Thomas Fortune, editor of the *New York Age*. Ida found out her *Free Speech* office had been destroyed by a mob on May 27, 1892, and a note was left threatening to kill Ida if she returned. "My friends declared that the trains and my home were being watched by white men who promised to kill me on sight."

Frederick Douglass's Letter to Ida

DEAR MISS WELLS:

Let me give you thanks for your faithful paper on the lynch abomination now generally practiced against colored people in the South. There has been no word equal to it in convincing power. I have spoken, but my word is feeble in comparison. You give us what you know and testify from actual knowledge. You have dealt with the facts with cool, painstaking fidelity and left those naked and uncontradicted facts to speak for themselves.

Brave woman! you have done your people and mine a service which can neither be weighed nor measured. If American conscience were only half alive, if the American church and clergy were only half Christianized, if American moral sensibility were not hardened by persistent infliction of outrage and crime against colored people, a scream of horror, shame and indignation would rise to Heaven wherever your pamphlet shall be read.

But alas! even crime has power to reproduce itself and create conditions favorable to its own existence. It sometimes seems we are deserted by earth and Heaven—yet we must still think, speak and work, and trust in the power of a merciful God for final deliverance.

Very truly and gratefully yours,
FREDERICK DOUGLASS
Cedar Hill, Anacostia, D.C., Oct. 25, 1892

START A WRITER'S CLUB

IDA B. WELLS WAS AN ACTIVE LEADER who liked to organize clubs so people could get together to talk, work on projects, or think about ways to help others.

Writers' clubs offer a fun way to spend time with friends while working on your writing skills. To organize a writer's club, decide where you'd like to meet, how often, and for how long. Think about how many people you would like to participate. It's often helpful to review your plans with adults or teachers to let them know what you have in mind and how they might be of help to you.

When you have a good idea of where you'd like to have your writer's club and how often you'll meet, come up with a name for your club.

Then, get the word out and see who's interested in participating. You could create a flyer, contact others via e-mail or social media, or announce the event through a school or community publication.

Once you have individuals who want to be in your writer's club, pick the types of writing assignments you'd like to work on. Would you like to write investigative newspaper articles? Short stories? Personal essays? Film scripts? Decide who will lead the group and if a different person will conduct different meetings, depending on the assignment. Set expectations for your writer's club so members understand what they'll be working on and what might be shared with the group in terms of helpful feedback.

Taking her friends' advice, Ida remained in New York and was hired by Fortune at the *New York Age* newspaper. She immediately began to investigate lynchings so she could write about these atrocities where people were hung, shot, knifed, or burned to death without fair trials for their alleged crimes. Ida was determined to figure out who was behind the lynchings and why the lynchings occurred.

As a writer at the *New York Age*, Ida was "given an opportunity to tell the world for the first time the true story of Negro lynchings, which were becoming more numerous and horrible." Although she'd been exiled from Memphis, Ida said, "I felt that I owed it to myself and my race to tell the whole truth."

Ida's article about lynching was published on June 25, 1892, and 10,000 copies circulated across America. People took notice, including Frederick Douglass, who was living in Washington, DC at the time. Douglass visited Ida in New York to tell her how her article had opened his eyes to lynchings. He then wrote a poignant preface to her pamphlet, *Southern Horrors: Lynch Law in All Its Phases*, published on October 26, 1892, by The New York Age Print.

THE POWER OF PEOPLE

AFTER READING Ida's article in the *New York Age*, many people wanted to hear from her directly, and Ida began speaking tours. She first spoke in Lyric Hall in Manhattan to a large crowd, giving an emotional, tear-filled account of the lynching of her friends. It was her first presentation before a major audience, and it led to many more speaking engagements throughout her life. Ida continued to speak out about lynching in many cities such as Boston, Philadelphia, and Washington, DC. She also went on two speaking tours in Europe to meet with the media and antilynching crusaders in England and Scotland who were very receptive to her message and eager to get the word out. In addition to talking about lynching, Ida told audiences about the conditions in the South after the Civil War and Reconstruction, including unfair racial segregation laws, intimidation, fraud in voting, and laws against interracial marriage.

When Ida was 31 years old, she headed to Chicago to attend the elaborate 1893 World's Fair, formally called the World's Columbian Exposition. When Ida found out the US government had refused African American participation in the event, she was incensed. The fair would have been an ideal venue to exhibit the many accomplishments of African Americans since the end of slavery. So, Ida took action. Along with social reformers Frederick Douglass, Irvine Garland Penn, and Ferdinand Lee Barnett, Ida helped write and distribute a pamphlet called *The Reason Why The Colored American is not in the*

On March 3, 1913, Ida marched for women's voting rights in Washington, DC.
Library of Congress LC-USZ62-22262

World's Columbian Exposition, with 10,000 copies published in English, French, and German. The pamphlet prompted World's Fair officials to sponsor a special day for African Americans; Douglass was asked to organize an event called Negro Day, which was well received.

In 1895 Ida married Ferdinand Barnett, and the couple raised four children. Ferdinand, an attorney and founder of *The Conservator*,

IDA B. WELLS liked to put her thoughts on paper. In addition to her journalistic writing, she kept a diary and wrote extensively for her autobiography. Keeping a journal can be an enjoyable way to write more frequently and to express yourself. Keep your journals and read them when you are older.

You'll Need

* Spiral notebook 6 by 9½ inches (15.2 by 24.1 cm)
* Construction paper
* Pencil
* Scissors
* Craft glue or glue stick
* Recycled magazines and newspapers
* Computer and printer (optional)
* Decorative paper and images
* Marker

1. Place the cover of the notebook over a piece of construction paper and trace around it.

2. Cut out the paper shape and glue it down over the notebook cover. Trim any excess paper.

3. Cut out images, words, and/or letters from recycled magazines or newspapers. You can also find and print online images.

4. Arrange decorative paper and images on your notebook cover, and glue them down.

5. You can also repeat steps 1–4 to cover the back of your journal.

6. It's a good idea to number or date your journal using a marker.

7. Remember—it's what's inside that counts. Begin to write! Not sure what to write about? Every journal is unique. You can:

* Keep a record of daily events in your life
* Write down article story ideas about things in your world you like, don't like, or would like to change
* Write about your feelings with poems, song lyrics, or personal essays
* Create lists of your favorite things
* Include quotes, mottos, drawings, photos, or images

Chicago's first African American newspaper, shared Ida's passion for civil rights. Although women's suffragist Susan B. Anthony chided Ida for getting married and having a "divided duty" that would take her away from her important civil rights work, Ida continued her lifelong crusade for social and political justice. She often worked with key people such as social reformer Jane Addams and civil rights activist W. E. B. Du Bois in her efforts toward social justice.

Ida also helped found a number of clubs and organizations, such as the Ida B. Wells Club in 1893, the National Association of Colored Women Clubs (NACWC) in 1896, and the National Association for the Advancement of Colored People (NAACP) in 1909. Ida also helped start the first African American women's suffrage organization, called the Alpha Suffrage Club, in 1913.

Ida B. Wells's life had changed dramatically when her parents died when she was only 16 years old. In her autobiography she wrote, "After being a happy, light-hearted schoolgirl, I suddenly found myself at the head of a family." But she took on the responsibility, paving the way for a lifetime of activism.

From Holly Springs to Memphis to New York City to Chicago, Ida B. Wells was a dynamic journalist who risked her life to fight injustice and bring more fairness and peace to the world. Today her legacy lives on via a number of Ida B. Wells high schools and scholarships and the Ida B. Wells Memorial Foundation.

Ida B. Wells's family portrait.
Special Collections Research Center, University of Chicago Library

*

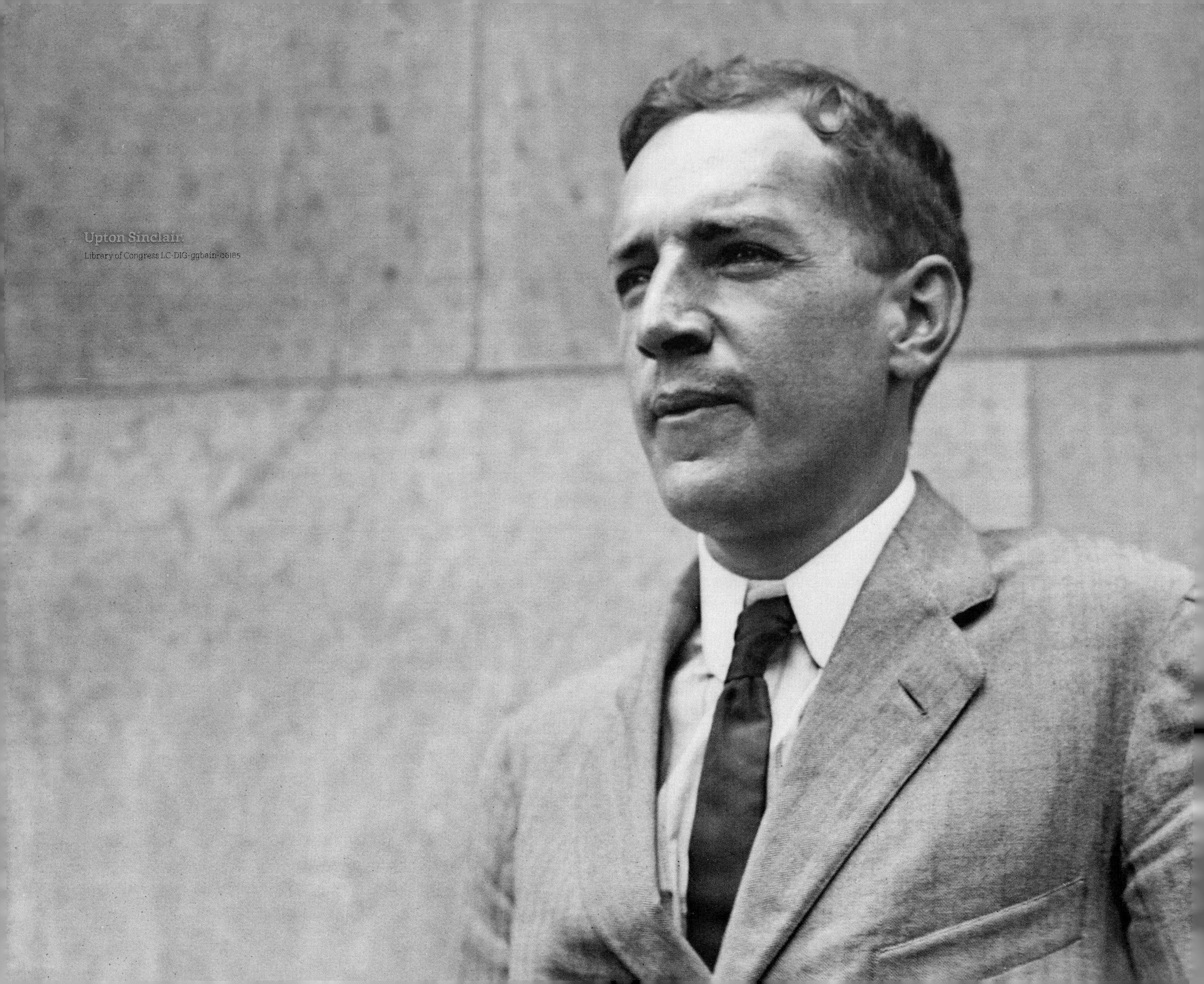

Upton Sinclair

Library of Congress LC-DIG-ggbain-06185

UPTON SINCLAIR

"For it was the custom, as they found, whenever meat was so spoiled that it could not be used for anything else, either to can it or else chop it up into sausage."

—Upton Sinclair

Upton Beall Sinclair Jr. (1878–1968) was a hardworking writer who poured a seemingly endless stream of words into nearly 90 books throughout his lifelong career as a freelance writer. As a muckraker, activist, and author, Upton presented many social reform issues through the stories, settings, and characters of his fictional novels. With fiction, he was able to tell original stories and capture the reader's attention in unique and riveting ways. Upton also wrote numerous nonfiction articles and books about social, political, and economic issues of his day.

Upton wrote about the changing world around him and explored a wide range of topics—everything from love to telepathy, coal to oil. His most famous work, *The Jungle*, was published by the time he was 28 years old and opened America's eyes to the horrors of the meatpacking industry in the early 1900s in Chicago. In 1919 he self-published *The Brass Check*, a nonfiction exposé of the American press that discusses issues such as censorship and yellow journalism. Twenty-four years later, Upton earned the Pulitzer Prize in 1943 for his historical novel *Dragon's Teeth*, which discusses the Nazi takeover of Germany in the 1930s before World War II.

As a young man, Upton was drawn to the social justice tenets of socialism, and he joined, quit, and rejoined the US Socialist Party at various times throughout his life. After moving to California, he founded the state's American Civil Liberties Union.

In addition to writing, Upton had political aspirations and ran, unsuccessfully, a number of times for various US offices on the Socialist or Democratic ticket.

BEDBUGS IN BALTIMORE

UPTON SINCLAIR was born in Baltimore, Maryland, on September 20, 1878, into a challenging and eccentric world of contrasts. His father, Upton Beall Sinclair Sr., was an alcoholic, while his mother, Priscilla Harden Beall, was the opposite and didn't drink alcoholic beverages. Although "both sides of his family came from the declining Southern aristocracy," Upton grew up in a world of poverty as well as wealth. His father's drinking "often caused the family to be impoverished."

An only child, Upton remembered early years of living in rundown boardinghouses where he and his parents lived together in one room. He would often sleep crossways at the foot of his parents' bed. Many nights when the gaslight was turned on, Upton would chase and mash cockroaches skittering about his sheets and blankets.

Upton's father was a drummer, a traveling salesman who drummed up business by selling wholesale whiskey or straw hats. Because of his work, the family moved regularly. Upton said living with an alcoholic father in a world of mint juleps, Scotch, and spiked punch was a "daily lesson in horror."

Upton grew up with wealth on his mother's side of the family. His maternal grandfather, John S. Harden, worked for the Western Maryland Railroad Company. As a boy Upton visited his grandfather's office at the railroad company and saw bags full of gold and silver coins that were used to pay the workers. His maternal aunt married Virginia statesman John Randolph Bland, who was one of the richest men in Baltimore. Upton regularly visited the Blands and spent summers in extravagant country homes or resorts. But he never felt comfortable in the wealthy world of plush surroundings and material possessions. He became an avid reader and found refuge from his chaotic childhood in books. He devoured classics such as *Gulliver's Travels*, the fairy tales of the Brothers Grimm, and the stories of Hans Christian Andersen.

MOVING NORTH

BEFORE UPTON was nine years old, his family moved to New York City. The Sinclairs lived in different parts of New York in tenement lodging houses, rundown hotels, small flats (apartments), and a family hotel that was not too far from the meatpacking district. Even though Upton lived in very modest residences, he enjoyed the excitement of big-city life and visiting the different neighborhoods that offered interesting adventures for a boy.

Upton taught himself how to read and became knowledgeable about many subjects. But he didn't go to school until he was 10. "When he was finally enrolled in public school, he was very advanced for his age—other than in arithmetic." He was told to go back to first grade to learn math. Humiliated by being a 10-year-old in a class with younger children, Upton studied hard and moved up quickly. He "went through

As a teen, Upton attended the College of the City of New York. Library of Congress LC-DIG-det-4a23361

eight years of grammar school in less than two years."

By 1892, when Upton was 14, he was enrolled at the College of the City of New York, which offered high school and college-level courses in subjects such as Latin, algebra, geometry, physics, drawing, and English. He didn't live close to the college, so he would take the train, walk, or ride his bike to school. Getting around in the city could be treacherous. Once when Upton was riding to school, his bike wheel slipped into a trolley slot and he was thrown right in front of an oncoming trolley car. Upton quickly rolled out of the way, causing a bystander to faint at his near miss.

Nonetheless, New York City offered plenty of fun for Upton, and Central Park was one of his favorite playgrounds. In Central Park, Upton ice-skated, sledded, threw snowballs, and played the running game of Hare and Hounds.

A TEENAGE AUTHOR

While in college, Upton's good friend Simon Stern published a short story in a monthly magazine. Upton was dazzled by the idea of being published and got right to work penning his own story about a pet bird that helped protect an African American boy wrongly accused of arson. Upton sent his story to the *Argosy* magazine, and editor Matthew White Jr. accepted the piece and paid him a whopping 25 dollars! Realizing his family could use the money, Upton found more freelance writing in "this new gold mine." He was soon earning money writing children's stories or sending one-dollar jokes to newspapers and magazines.

Upton and Simon later became writing partners and wrote a dime novel for Street & Smith Publishing in one week. Dime novels, also called potboilers, were a form of popular pulp fiction featuring romance or adventure tales. Unfortunately, the Street & Smith editors were not impressed with the boys' hastily written novel.

The next summer Upton wrote an adventure novel titled *The Prairie Pirates* he later admitted was a rehash of Robert Louis Stevenson's *Treasure Island*. His career in writing was taking

Like these children who are sledding, Upton had a lot of fun in New York City's Central Park.
Library of Congress LC-USZ62-111106

off, but he was in the middle of college studies and ongoing challenges with his alcoholic father. His father, whose drinking had worsened, would disappear for days, forcing Upton to search for him in New York City barrooms, begging him to come home. Upton said this miserable routine made him "prematurely serious." It also prompted him to question the world and its many vices and influenced his future work as an investigative journalist.

After graduating from the College of the City of New York in 1897, Upton thought about going to law school. Instead, he took literature and philosophy courses at Columbia University in the city and focused on his writing. Although Upton was younger than Nellie Bly, Jacob Riis, Ida Tarbell, and Ida B. Wells, it was likely that he was reading and perhaps was inspired by their social reform writing in newspaper and magazine articles as well as books.

But in 1897, Upton was focused on earning money to support himself. He returned to Street & Smith to inquire about work and was hired as a freelancer to write 25,000-word novelettes about the West Point Military Academy for the publisher's new five-cent *Army and Navy Weekly* publication. Upton was thrilled. Using the pen name Lieutenant Frederick Garrison, USA, Upton's first piece was about West Point cadets. The editors loved the story and it was a hit. Upton was paid $40 for the story, which was

WRITE A SHORT STORY "MUCKRAKER" STYLE

INSPIRING STORIES about socially conscious issues are sometimes told through the short story structure. Short stories typically revolve around one main character who is up against a difficult situation and needs to find a way out or solve a problem. Try your hand at writing a short story about a personal, social, or political issue that concerns you.

You'll Need
* Pencil or pen
* Writing paper

1. Think about a topic for your story and an issue you'd like to write about. You may want to check out the news for story ideas or find real-life stories around your hometown. Jot down a few ideas on a piece of paper and then decide on your topic.

2. Next, decide on a main character for your story. Choose a name for your character and write down a few characteristics about this individual, such as the character's age and where he or she lives.

3. Think about one or two secondary characters who will interact with your main character. Are they friends? Enemies? Give them names and describe them in writing.

4. Now, come up with a problem or issue your main character faces in your story. You may wish to write a short outline that provides a beginning, middle, and end for your story and addresses the theme. Create a title

5. You may want to conduct investigative research to learn more about your topic. You can find research materials at places such as a library, your school, or online. It's up to you. You might even want to interview someone who knows about your topic.

6. Now it's time to write your story, which can be anywhere from about 200 to 1,000 words or more. It's often good to include dialogue in your story to give your characters a voice.

7. After you've written your short story, read it out loud for yourself or someone else.

8. You can also revise and rewrite your story if you so choose.

a lot of money for the time. He used the money to help out his family.

Shortly after this, Street & Smith editors wanted Upton to focus his stories on the Spanish-American War that had just started on April 25, 1898. "Willie Hearst with his *New York Evening Journal* succeeded in carrying the United States into a war with Spain," Upton wrote in his autobiography. Upton's West Point characters were now to graduate from the academy and head straight to the battlefields in Cuba to fight the Spaniards.

The editors were pleased with Upton's writing and continued to give him more assignments. At times, with the aid of stenographers, he was writing 8,000 words a day! Upton admittedly described this fast and furious writing as hackwork, which began to bore him. He eventually became obsessed with wanting to write a serious, more poignant novel that would sell. For inspiration, Upton started to venture out into the woods near Maryland or to the lake and river regions of northern New York and Canada. His mind overflowed with ideas in the beauty of these natural settings.

He wrote and self-published his first novel, a love story titled *Springtime and Harvest*, in 1901 when he was 23. The following year Upton married a Virginia childhood friend, Meta Fuller, and they had a son named David. Over the next five years, Upton published five more books, which paved the way for his most famous, best-selling novel.

THE JUNGLE

LIKE OTHER muckrakers of the Progressive Era, Upton became interested in writing about the problems of society and reform. As his interests changed, he started to meet individuals who influenced his direction in life as well as his writing.

In 1902, Upton met Leonard D. Abbott, an art editor working for the *Literary Digest* magazine in New York. Leonard introduced him to the socialism movement in the United States and gave him pamphlets to read. Upton was drawn to the philosophies of socialism—a political and economic system urging collective or government ownership and distribution of goods—which spoke to his deep-felt desires for more equity between the rich and poor in society.

Upton started to write articles for the socialist newspaper *Appeal to Reason*. Fred Warren, an editor for the paper, was impressed with Upton's work and asked him to write about how some workers were treated poorly, exploited, and underpaid in the United States. Upton was up for the task and decided to focus on the meatpacking laborers of Chicago. The assignment changed his life.

Excerpt from *The Jungle*

There were men who worked in the cooking-rooms, in the midst of steam and sickening odors, by artificial light; in these rooms the germs of tuberculosis might live for two years, but the supply was renewed every hour. There were the beef-luggers, who carried two-hundred-pound quarters into the refrigerator-cars; a fearful kind of work, that began at four o'clock in the morning, and that wore out the most powerful men in a few years. There were those who worked in the chilling-rooms, and whose special disease was rheumatism; the time-limit that a man could work in the chilling rooms was said to be five years. There were the wool-pluckers, whose hands went to pieces even sooner than the hands of the pickle-men; for the pelts of sheep had to be painted with acid to loosen the wool, and then the pluckers had to pull out this wool with their bare hands, till the acid had eaten their fingers off.

Upton's famous book *The Jungle* influenced reforms in meatpacking operations in America. In this 1906 photo, Chicago meatpackers split the backbones of hogs in preparation for market. Library of Congress LC-USZ62-55730

UNDERCOVER AND OVERWHELMED

LIKE NELLIE Bly, who had gone undercover to write about the abuses of a women's insane asylum, Upton Sinclair went undercover in the Chicago stockyards. What he found there was utterly disturbing.

For seven weeks Upton lived among the workers in the stockyards, listening to their stories and taking careful notes. He dressed like a worker and carried a lunch pail so he could move easily and undetected throughout the factories and yards. It was hard work and Upton often felt ill and lost his appetite. He observed men in pickling rooms with crippled backs, respiratory diseases, skin sores, and lost fingers. He was sickened when he saw sausage meat piled up on the floor and riddled with rat dung, spit, and urine. He observed that so-called chicken was sometimes a mystery meat mixture of pork and beef scraps.

When Upton returned to his home in New Jersey after about two months, he got straight

SEND A LETTER TO YOUR FUTURE SELF

UPTON SINCLAIR WROTE many letters to friends and family throughout his life. Even though e-mail and texting are popular today, letter writing is still an interesting way to record and share your thoughts with others. It's fun to read letters you've written earlier in your life to see how you've changed or to reminisce about what you were doing at an earlier time in your life. In this activity you'll write a letter to yourself that will, ideally, not be opened for 10 years.

You'll Need
* Pencil or pen
* Writing paper
* Envelope
* Stamp

1. Write down your current age and then add 10 years. This is when you'll reread this letter.

2. On writing paper, address your letter to yourself. Or you might write, "Dear Future Self."

3. The content of your letter will be unique, but here are a few suggestions. You can describe where you live, what you look like now, your friends, and your favorite activities. You can write about what you're studying in school and ideas for a future career. You can reveal what makes you happy or angry. It's all up to you.

4. Once you've completed your letter, fold it and place it in an envelope. You might want to include a photo of yourself.

5. Address the letter to yourself at your home address; the return address should also be your home address. On the outside of the letter write, "Don't open until 2025," or whatever year is 10 years from when you send it.

6. Make sure you have enough stamps for the letter's weight and size. Then, put it in a mailbox.

7. When you receive your letter, put it in a safe place.

8. In 10 years, open the letter and enjoy reading about your life way back when.

to work. He felt a great deal of anguish putting down the words on paper. The memories of the meatpacking factory dredged up tears and sadness and reminded him of pain he'd felt in his life.

His manuscript, titled *The Jungle*, told the story of the Chicago stockyards through the eyes of a fictional main character, Jurgis Rudkus, a Lithuanian immigrant trying to create a better life in America for his new bride, Ona. In the book, Jurgis is employed at Brown's Slaughterhouse in Chicago, where the conditions are harsh. Over time, the young couple's life becomes a deadly nightmare.

Upton first published segments of *The Jungle* in the *Appeal to Reason* magazine. To publicize the upcoming series, he wrote, "It will set forth the breaking of human hearts in a system which exploits the labor of men and women for profits. It will shake the popular heart and blow the top off of the industrial tea-kettle."

He then sent the manuscript to publishers with the hopes of it becoming a book. The novel was turned down by five publishers but finally published by Doubleday, Page & Company in February 1906. When *The Jungle* came out in book form, it shocked readers. Upton had set out to write about the abuse of workers, but readers reacted to the unsanitary conditions of the stockyards and the unhealthy meat products they were potentially purchasing, eating, and feeding to their children.

Many people, including President Theodore Roosevelt, read *The Jungle* and were very concerned about what Upton had written. Roosevelt invited the young author to meet with him at the White House to discuss *The Jungle*, and the book was an important element in the passing of the Pure Food and Drug Act of 1906 and the Federal Meat Inspection Act of 1906.

Upton was a social crusader who died in his sleep at the age of 90 in New Jersey. He wrote steadily throughout his life and never seemed to tire of coming up with ideas, conducting research, and speaking out through his writing. In addition to his novels, he wrote about diverse subjects including birth control, child labor, civil liberties, economics, education reform, health and health care, journalism, politics, prohibition, socialism, spiritualism, telepathy, trade unions, and vegetarianism.

Upton's many books have been published in major languages throughout the world. His writing has been praised as well as criticized, and he is often remembered as a "rebel with a cause" who fought for the underdog. In his November 26, 1968, obituary, the *New York Times* wrote, "Mr. Sinclair's weapon was his pen, and few writers wielded it so tellingly in battles against the social and economic ills of the United States."

✳

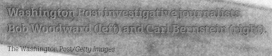

MODERN-DAY MUCKRAKERS

*"How lovely to think that no one need wait a moment,
we can start now, start slowly changing the world!"*

—ANNE FRANK

Ever since President Theodore Roosevelt first coined the label *muck-raker* in 1906, investigative journalists have continued to bring stories about wrongdoing to light. Early muckrakers wrote articles in newspapers and magazines and published books. With advances in technology, journalists turned toward the radio, television, film, and the Internet to reach mass audiences with their stories. Some modern-day muckrakers have changed the course of history.

Every day, journalists continue to unearth new stories and shed light on issues we need to think about and possibly change. Here are a few examples of modern-day muckrakers.

AMY GOODMAN

Amy Goodman. Courtesy Democracy Now!

"We need a media that provides a forum for people to speak for themselves."

—AMY GOODMAN

AMY GOODMAN is an award-winning American journalist, author, syndicated columnist, and the host of the acclaimed international news program *Democracy Now!* She believes in the power of independent media and has been an investigative journalist nearly her entire life. In addition to her reporting in the United States, Amy has covered important stories all over the world, in countries such as East Timor, Nigeria, Peru, and Haiti.

While growing up in Bay Shore, New York, she wrote editorials for her high school newspaper. She also watched her brother, David Goodman, create *Dave's Press*, a publication headquartered in his bedroom that discussed everything from family matters to politics.

After graduating from Radcliffe College in 1984 with a degree in anthropology, Amy volunteered at WBAI community radio in New York City, which is part of the noncommercial Pacifica Radio Network. She was eventually promoted to WBAI news director and produced the evening news for a decade.

In 1996, Pacifica asked Amy to host a daily election show, which was broadcast to community radio stations across the country. This well-received show was the start of *Democracy Now!*, which has grown rapidly over the years and now airs on more than 1,000 public television and radio stations globally, including Public Broadcasting Service (PBS) stations, satellite TV, and public access television, with a growing Internet audience at democracynow.org.

Amy is executive producer of *Democracy Now!* and co-hosts the news program with award-winning journalist Juan González. She is the co-author of five bestselling books (three books were co-written with David Goodman; one book was co-written with colleague Denis Moynihan).

Amy has received many awards over the years. She was the first journalist to receive the Right Livelihood Award (2008), known as the Alternative Nobel Prize, for her work as an independent journalist. She received the Gandhi Peace Award (2012) for her contributions to international peace, and co-received the Park Center for Independent Media Izzy Award (2009), named after the American muckraking journalist I. F. Stone.

The Watergate Scandal

A DRAMATIC and historic example of modern-day muckraking occurred in the early 1970s. Bob Woodward and Carl Bernstein, two reporters from the *Washington Post* newspaper, covered the Watergate political scandal involving Richard Nixon (the 37th US President, from 1969 to 1974).

During the presidential election campaign of 1972, police caught and arrested five men who had broken into the headquarters of the Democratic National Committee (DNC), located in the Watergate Hotel in Washington, DC. The five men were attempting to illegally plant listening devices in the DNC office. Sensing there was a bigger story behind the Watergate break-in, journalists Woodward and Bernstein worked tirelessly to uncover the details. There were many roadblocks. People they tried to interview didn't want to talk, and Woodward and Bernstein relied on an anonymous source known as Deep Throat to piece together the story that led all the way to the US Justice Department, FBI, CIA, and ultimately the White House.

Republican incumbent Richard Nixon was reelected as president on November 7, 1972, but after the continual exposure of unethical practices during his presidency, Nixon resigned on August 8, 1974.

In 2005, William Mark Felt, associate director at the FBI during the Watergate scandal, revealed he was the Deep Throat whistleblower.

Washington Post investigative journalists Bob Woodward (left) and Carl Bernstein (right) exposed government corruption in their articles about the Watergate break-in. The Washington Post/Getty Images

MICHAEL MOSS

"My goal as a reporter is to help people make healthier choices and to have more control over their lives."

—Michael Moss

Michael Moss is a Pulitzer Prize–winning investigative journalist who has taken on giants in his reporting. Food industry giants, to be exact.

His bestselling book, *Salt Sugar Fat: How the Food Giants Hooked Us*, sheds light on the US food industry and the many processed ingredients we eat that could dangerously affect our health.

Michael grew up in different towns in central California and enjoyed frequent trips to the library as a boy. He liked to read books such as

Michael Moss. Tony Cenicola/the *New York Times*

The *Diary of Anne Frank* and stories about American frontiersman Kit Carson. As a teen, Michael was very interested in the news. He read the local *Fresno Bee* newspaper and watched the nightly television news, which was often about the Vietnam War, with his family.

At Lowell High School in San Francisco, Michael's journalism teacher saw promise in his writing. Although Michael thought writing was difficult, this inspired him to pursue journalism. While at Lowell, he started to sell freelance articles to local weekly newspapers.

After studying journalism at San Francisco State University, Michael landed reporting jobs with the Pacific News Service and the Sierra Club in San Francisco. From California he moved to Wyoming, where he reported for the *High Country News*. Michael then went to work for many papers across the country, including the *Wall Street Journal* in New York City, New York's, *Newsday*, and the *Atlanta Journal-Constitution*.

Since 2000, Michael has worked for the *New York Times* as a reporter with the investigations group. He believes in the importance of investigative journalism and said, "We need investigative reporting to expose wrongdoing and problems that otherwise nobody would know about."

Eye on the Investigative Prize

The Pulitzer Prizes for Investigative Reporting have been awarded to journalists since 1964 through the Columbia University Graduate School of Journalism in New York City. Journalists win awards for their writing about issues such as abuses of power, corruption in government, unsafe prescription drugs, voter fraud, medical malpractice, urban problems, clandestine spying, toxic ingredients, the freeing of wrongly convicted prisoners, and much more. To find out more about these awards, go to: www.pulitzer.org/bycat/Investigative-Reporting.

ANNIE LEONARD

"Have you ever wondered where all the stuff we buy comes from and where it goes when we throw it out? I couldn't stop wondering about that."

—ANNIE LEONARD

THROWN-OUT PLASTIC bottles, bags, boxes, cans, and other kinds of garbage—you name it, Annie Leonard has obsessed about it. But she hasn't stopped there.

As an environmentalist activist and writer, Annie has spent decades traveling to countries such as Haiti, Bangladesh, India, and South Africa to figure out how stuff is manufactured, distributed, and disposed of. Her work has translated to films, a book, and podcasts.

During her worldwide investigations, she visited all sorts of factories and garbage dumps to find out what was really going on. After conducting firsthand research, she wrote and narrated *The Story of Stuff*, a popular, award-winning 2007 Internet film, to help people realize the consequences of consumerism. In addition, Annie published *The Story of Stuff* book in 2010.

She is now the director of The Story of Stuff Project headquartered in Berkeley, California, and is on the board of environmental groups such as the Global Alliance for Incinerator Alternatives (GAIA), and the consumer rights group Public Citizen.

Annie grew up in Seattle, Washington, and earned a master's degree in city and regional planning from Cornell University. During her studies at Cornell, she interned at the National Wildlife Federation in Washington, DC, which led to a job at Greenpeace, a global environmental organization. At Greenpeace, she was assigned to investigate international waste dumping. Her work contributed to the formation of the Basel Convention, an international treaty enacted in 1992 to prevent the transfer of hazardous waste from developed to less-developed countries.

Annie Leonard has many important stories to tell. She has also helped create more Internet films, including *The Story of Solutions*, *The Story of Electronics*, *The Story of Bottled Water*, and *The Story of Cosmetics*.

Annie Leonard. Photo credit Lindsay France, Cornell University

BILL MOYERS

Bill Moyers. Peter Krogh

"Exploration is the key."

—Bill Moyers

Bill Moyers is one of the most recognized and acclaimed American broadcast journalists of our time. During his 40-year run on public television, he won many Emmy Awards for his television shows and investigative documentaries. In 2001, his two-hour television special, *Trade Secrets*, investigated the chemical industry in America and the potential dangers of chemicals in our foods, products, and everyday life.

Bill Moyers grew up in the small town of Marshall, Texas, and began his career in journalism as a teenager when he was a junior reporter at the local *Marshall News Messenger* newspaper. He graduated from the University of Texas at Austin in 1956 with a degree in journalism and received his Master of Divinity degree from Southwestern Baptist Theological Seminary in Texas.

His interest in politics and journalism took him to Washington, DC, in the early 1960s, where he became a founding organizer and deputy director of the Peace Corps, as well as a special assistant and press secretary to Lyndon B. Johnson, the 36th US President.

In 1967, Bill left Washington, DC, and became publisher of the daily newspaper *Newsday* on Long Island. He then joined PBS in New York City in 1971, starting his long career as a TV producer and host.

He and his wife and creative partner, Judith Davidson Moyers, have produced acclaimed television series such as *Healing and the Mind*, *Joseph Campbell and the Power of Myth*, *A World of Ideas*, and the weekly television series, *Now with Bill Moyers*, and the *Bill Moyers Journal*. They currently produce the weekly television interview series *Moyers & Company*, which began in January 2012.

Bill Moyers is president of the Schumann Media Center, a nonprofit organization for the support of independent journalism. In 2006, the National Academy of Television Arts and Sciences presented Bill with a Lifetime Achievement Award for devoting his life to exploring major issues and ideas of our time.

TAKE A CLOSER LOOK

A WIDE RANGE OF STORIES comes to us through print, broadcast, and Internet venues that cater to all sorts of views, interests, and concerns. The journalists behind these stories have different roles—they might present, report on, comment on, or investigate the news. Thousands of journalists are at work every day, and each individual has a unique voice. In this activity you can learn about various journalists, think about their different roles, and consider what interests you.

You'll Need
* Computer (optional)
* Pencil or pen
* Writing paper

1. Read through the following list of different types of journalists, and go online or visit a library to learn more about some of them. You can research topics such as what they studied in school, where they landed their first job, where they currently work, and what articles or books they may have written.

Christiane Amanpour (CNN, ABC television anchor)

Ed Bradley (*60 Minutes* TV show anchor)

Caroline Baum (*Bloomberg News* columnist)

David Brooks (*New York Times* op-ed columnist)

Rachel Carson (author, *Silent Spring*)

Walter Cronkite (CBS *Evening News* anchor)

Anderson Cooper (CNN anchor)

Barbara Ehrenreich (author, *Nickel and Dimed*)

Charles Krauthammer (political commentator, columnist)

Glenn Greenwald (political journalist)

Terry Gross ("Fresh Air" radio show host)

Sean Hannity (Fox News television host)

Diana B. Henriques (*New York Times* reporter)

Seymour Hersh (investigative journalist)

Laura Ingraham (radio talk show host)

Molly Ivins (*Fort Worth Star-Telegram* columnist)

Clifford J. Levy (*New York Times* investigative journalist)

Michael Moore (political activist, filmmaker)

Edward R. Murrow (World War II broadcast journalist)

Ralph Nader (consumer advocate, author, *Unsafe at Any Speed*)

Scott Pelley (*60 Minutes* television anchor)

Dana Priest (*Washington Post* investigative reporter)

Diane Sawyer (ABC news anchor)

Eric Schlosser (author, *Fast Food Nation*)

Tavis Smiley (PBS television show host)

Morgan Spurlock (filmmaker, *Super Size Me*)

Gloria Steinem (*Ms. Magazine* cofounder)

I. F. Stone (investigative journalist)

George Will (*Washington Post* columnist)

Oprah Winfrey (television show host)

2. Think about which journalists you consider to be modern-day muckrakers.

3. After you've researched a few journalists on this list, you might like to take a closer look at their work by watching their broadcasts or films, reading their writing, or following their careers. Be sure a parent or guardian OKs your choices.

BE A FILM CRITIC

MANY MOVIES and documentaries present stories about social consciousness and social reform issues. A few examples include *Norma Rae* about workers' rights, *A Place at the Table* about hunger in the United States, and *To Kill a Mockingbird* about racial inequality.

Reviewing a film can be a way to express your thoughts and opinions through writing. Instead of simply watching a film, you take on the role of the observer and critic. In this activity you'll write down your thoughts about a film and shape them into a review.

You'll Need
* Movie
* Pencil or pen
* Writing paper
* Computer and printer (optional)

1. Watch a movie about an issue that concerns you. Check with your parents, library, or school, or go online to find a movie you might want to watch that's age appropriate. Be sure a parent or guardian OKs your choice.

2. As you watch the film, take a few notes to help you remember important details.

3. The length of your review is up to you, but it could be approximately 100–300 words.

4. Include the title of the film, followed by names of key people who helped produce the movie, including the producer, director, screenwriter, and main actors.

5. Summarize what the film is about and what happens in the story. You can think about the 5Ws (who, what, when, where, why) to help structure this part of your review. Try not to give away the ending.

6. Next, write about why you liked or didn't like the film. Be as specific as possible. Was the movie easy or difficult to follow? Were you bored or thrilled watching the film? Did you like the music? What age group would like this film?

7. To conclude your review, indicate whether you recommend the film or not.

8. Proofread your review and correct any mistakes in it.

9. If you'd like, try submitting your review to a school or local newspaper for publication, or share it with your family and friends.

MOVING FORWARD

JOURNALISM HAS continued to evolve for many reasons, including changes in society, technology, and humankind. In recent years, for example, the computer and social media have played a big part in how print, broadcast, and Internet stories reach audiences and how reporters gather and present information.

Be curious about your world. Ask questions. Think about stories you'd like to tell or instances where you'd like to see change. There will always be a need for passionate, hardworking reporters like Nellie Bly and the many journalists featured in this book to investigate stories, seek the truth, and make a positive difference in the world. Perhaps one day you will be a journalist.

✳

What Is a Whistleblower?

MUCKRAKERS EXPOSE wrongdoing and sometimes rely on whistleblowers to get information for their stories. A whistleblower is an individual who witnesses misconduct (in a workplace, for example) and then decides to "blow the whistle" on an individual or organization he or she perceives is wrong. Although there are laws to protect whistleblowers, these individuals often take risks and put themselves in harm's way. The consequences of whistleblowing can be both negative and positive.

Here are a few well-known whistleblowers:

✳ In 2013, whistleblower Edward Snowden, a former CIA employee and contractor for the National Security Agency (NSA), decided to inform the public about the agency's spying via technology such as phones and computers. Snowden leaked thousands of classified NSA computer documents to several media outlets and has been both criticized and praised for his whistleblowing; he is viewed as both a traitor and a hero.

✳ In 1993, single mother Erin Brockovich blew the whistle and helped win a lawsuit against the Pacific Gas and Electric Company in California (PG&E). Brockovich exposed how PG&E was poisoning the water supply in the town of Hinkley, California, which affected the health of hundreds of Hinkley residents. Her true story was produced as a major motion picture in 2000 titled *Erin Brockovich*.

✳ In 1971, whistleblower Daniel Ellsberg, a former US military analyst of the RAND Corporation, leaked secret government documents known as the Pentagon Papers about the Vietnam War, which were published in the *New York Times*. These documents influenced the end of the Vietnam War.

ACKNOWLEDGMENTS

I'd like to thank my editor, Lisa Reardon, and everyone at Chicago Review Press for helping me bring this book to light for young readers. I'm also very appreciative of the following individuals who helped with research and review of the manuscript: Marilyn Black, Dan Duster, Ruth Engs, Tri Fritz, Karen Kimball, Cristine Kostiuk, Brooke Kroeger, Joseph O. Legaspi, Kathy McCardwell, Michael Moss, Denis Moynihan, Mary Mark Ockerbloom, Caitlin Oriel, Sue Ott, Patricia Schechter, Paula Treckel, Erika Stutzman, Paul Voakes, Bill Walker, and Bonnie Yochelson. I would also like to thank the helpful reference staff of the Library of Congress, the Boulder History Museum, and the Ida B. Wells-Barnett Museum.

✻

Courtesy Rob Niederman

113

RESOURCES

PLACES TO VISIT

Lower East Side Tenement Museum
103 Orchard Street
New York, NY 10002
(877) 975-3786
www.tenement.org
Take a walking tour to explore New York City's Lower East Side and the American immigrant experience.

National Women's Hall of Fame
76 Fall Street
Seneca Falls, NY 13148
(315) 568-8060
www.greatwomen.org
This Hall of Fame selects and honors women on the basis of the changes they helped bring about that affect social, economic, or cultural aspects of society.

Newseum (Washington, DC)
555 Pennsylvania Avenue N.W.
Washington, DC 20001
(888) NEWSEUM / (888) 639-7386
www.newseum.org
This interactive museum features journalism and news and highlights high-tech as well as historic information about the US press.

WEBSITES TO INVESTIGATE

A Celebration of Women Writers

http://digital.library.upenn.edu/women/writers
.html

Edited by Mary Mark Ockerbloom in collaboration with the University of Pennsylvania Digital Library, this website offers links to books and articles by women writers. Search for Nellie Bly to find some of her original works.

The Center for Investigative Reporting

http://cironline.org

A California-based online news organization focused on investigative reporting.

Center for Public Integrity

www.publicintegrity.org

Founded by investigative journalist Charles Lewis, the CPI is a nonpartisan investigative news organization.

**Ida B. Wells Papers 1884–1976—
University of Chicago Library**

www.lib.uchicago.edu/e/scrc/findingaids/view
.php?eadid=ICU.SPCL.IBWELLS

A collection of Ida B. Wells's manuscripts, articles, and speeches.

**Ida M. Tarbell Collection—
Allegheny College Special Collections**

http://library.allegheny.edu/content.php?pid
=57261&sid=419389

The professional papers, manuscripts, research papers, and correspondence of Ida M. Tarbell.

I-News Rocky Mountain PBS

http://inewsnetwork.org/

A Colorado-based PBS show offering viewers investigative broadcast stories.

IRE—Investigative Reporters & Editors

www.ire.org

Located at the Missouri School of Journalism, this organization fosters excellence in investigative journalism with resources, training, and conferences for journalists.

Jacob Riis—Museum of the City of New York

http://collections.mcny.org/Explore/Highlights/
Jacob%20A.%20Riis/

A vast collection of Riis's photographs he used in his writing and lecturing.

**The National Women's History Museum
Presents: Women with a Deadline**

www.nwhm.org/online-exhibits/womenwith
deadlines/wwd1.htm

An exceptional online exhibit that highlights the role of women in the American press from the 17th-century "Pioneers of the Press" to the yellow journalists and muckrakers of the early 1900s. The NWHM was founded in 1996 as an inspiring way to present women's distinct historic and cultural achievements in the United States.

Nellie Bly of The New York World

http://dlib.nyu.edu/undercover/nellie-bly-new
-york-world-0

This link features *New York World* articles penned by Nellie Bly.

Nellie Bly: Online Resources

www.loc.gov/rr/program/bib/bly

Compiled by Kathryn Funk, this comprehensive, easy-to-use Library of Congress website includes a helpful bibliography and wide array of links to websites related to Nellie Bly, her works, and her life and times.

Nellie Bly—The Pioneer Woman Journalist

www.nellieblyonline.com

An excellent, visually dynamic website about Nellie Bly that includes biographical information, examples of Nellie's writing, a photo gallery, and links to books and websites. The website, created by author and Nellie Bly historian Tri Fritz, is easy to navigate.

Society of Professional Journalists

www.spj.org

Headquartered in Indianapolis, Indiana, SPJ is one of the oldest professional organizations for journalists, offering helpful resources, journalism job listings, and a journalist's code of ethics.

Undercover Reporting—
Deception for Journalism's Sake: A Database

http://dlib.nyu.edu/undercover

Created by author and New York University journalism professor Brooke Kroeger in collaboration with NYU Libraries, this website presents a fascinating database of journalistic works (predominantly from the United States) that used undercover techniques.

Upton Sinclair (1878–1968)—
The Lilly Library, Indiana University

www.indiana.edu/~liblilly/collections/overview/
    sinclair.shtml

An extensive collection of the manuscripts and letters of Upton Sinclair.

✳

"f I gits married I got ter hustle if I nts ter keep de wolf away furninst door."

"I'm stuck on der perleece, an' I tink I could do it, 'cause bein' a cop is dead easy."

"Composin' music dese days is easy; all yer have ter do is ter buy Gilbert and Sullivan and de 'Chimes of Normandy' an' yez kin rite an opera."

"I might earn some money on shakin' de bones."

NOTES

Introduction

"Energy rightly applied" Bly, *Among the Mad*, 20

Chapter 1

"all was calm" Kroeger, *Nellie Bly*, 4.
"justice of the peace in 1840" Kroeger, *Nellie Bly*, 3.
"doctor, a dentist" Macy, *Bylines*, 8.
"a mean and abusive drunk" Kroeger, *Nellie Bly*, 15.
"My age is 14" Kroeger, *Nellie Bly*, 20.
"[I have] seen mother vexed" Kroeger, *Nellie Bly*, 20.
"monstrosity" Kroeger, *Nellie Bly*, 37.
"there is no greater abnormity" Kroeger, *Nellie Bly*, 37.
"If the writer of the communication" Kroeger, *Nellie Bly*, 39.

Chapter 2

"I was too" Fritz, *Nellie Bly Collection*, 189.
"Three days" Fritz, *Nellie Bly Collection*, 189.
"At a fight" Fritz, *Nellie Bly Collection*, 217.
"Butter is" Fritz, *Nellie Bly Collection*, 325.

"Jalapa has" Fritz, *Nellie Bly Collection*, 266.
"the worst" Fritz, *Nellie Bly Collection*, 292.
"I am off" Kroeger, *Nellie Bly*, 75.
"I said I could" Fritz, *Nellie Bly Collection*, 17.
"What a difficult task," Fritz, *Nellie Bly Collection*, 19.
"I began to think" Fritz, *Nellie Bly Collection*, 19.
"It was a wretchedly" Fritz, *Nellie Bly Collection*, 23.
"The insane asylum" Fritz, *Nellie Bly Collection*, 70.
"I was to chronicle" Fritz, *Nellie Bly Collection*, 17.
"Suddenly I got" Fritz, *Nellie Bly Collection*, 50.
"We were compelled," Fritz, *Nellie Bly Collection*, 53.

Chapter 3

"two traveling caps" Fritz, *Nellie Bly Collection*, 80.
"I felt lost" Fritz, *Nellie Bly Collection*, 82.
"I slept an easy" Fritz, *Nellie Bly Collection*, 91.
"I went out on the platform" Fritz, *Nellie Bly Collection*, 102.

"a stick beats" Fritz, *Nellie Bly Collection*, 111.

"Here's Gladstone!" Fritz, *Nellie Bly Collection*, 112.

"Hong Kong is" Fritz, *Nellie Bly Collection*, 148.

"I promised my editor" Fritz, *Nellie Bly Collection*, 151.

"cleaned-up" Fritz, *Nellie Bly Collection*, 167.

"The face is" Fritz, *Nellie Bly Collection*, 170.

"My feverish eagerness" Fritz, *Nellie Bly Collection*, 175.

"For Nellie Bly" Fritz, *Nellie Bly Collection*, 175.

"I only remember" Fritz, *Nellie Bly Collection*, 179.

"F. W. Stevens" Macy, *Bylines*, 46.

"Nellie Bly was" Macy, *Bylines*, 57.

Chapter 4

"it has become" Douglas, *The Golden Age of the Newspaper*, 110.

"Now, it is very" Roosevelt, *Voices of Democracy*, 3.

"There should be" Roosevelt, *Voices of Democracy*, 7.

Chapter 5

"The half that was on top" Riis, *How the Other Half Lives*, 6.

"stories ever so much" Riis, *The Making of an American*, 4.

"I kissed her hands" Riis, *The Making of an American*, 32.

"I lived on that picture" Riis, *The Making of an American*, 33.

"I had a pair" Riis, *The Making of an American*, 35.

"It was a beautiful spring morning" Riis, *The Making of an American*, 35.

"I walked till the stars" Riis, *The Making of an American*, 52.

"joined the great army" Riis, *The Making of an American*, 66.

"Raving like a madman" Riis, *The Making of an American*, 73.

"Is that the way" Riis, *The Making of an American*, 195.

"You can run there" Riis, *The Making of an American*, 197.

Chapter 6

"Go away" Tarbell, *All in the Day's Work*, 3.

"My first reaction" Tarbell, *All in the Day's Work*, 5.

"Respect for my mother" Tarbell, *All in the Day's Work*, 6.

"fountain wells" Tarbell, *All in the Day's Work*, 8.

"No industry of man" Tarbell, *All in the Day's Work*, 9.

"producing some" Tarbell, *All in the Day's Work*, 23.

"O Liberty!" Abbott, *Madame Roland*, 300.

"You're not a writer" Tarbell, *All in the Day's Work*, 87.

"The deluge of" Tarbell, *All in the Day's Work*, 202.

"Feeling as I did" Tarbell, *All in the Day's Work*, 327.

Chapter 7

"Our job was to" Duster, *Crusade for Justice*, 9.

"He was interested" Duster, *Crusade for Justice*, 9.

"plain, common-sense" Duster, *Crusade for Justice*, 24.

"The correspondence" Duster, *Crusade for Justice*, 31.

"Iola" Duster, *Crusade for Justice*, 33.

"Our [*Free Speech*] circulation" Duster, *Crusade for Justice*, 41.

"He [Thomas] owned" Duster, *Crusade for Justice*, 48.

"The men" Duster, *Crusade for Justice*, 49.

"Negroes shooting" Duster, *Crusade for Justice*, 49.

"Over a hundred" Duster, *Crusade for Justice*, 49.

"My friends" Duster, *Crusade for Justice*, 62.

"given an opportunity" Duster, *Crusade for Justice*, 63.

"I felt" Duster, *Crusade for Justice*, 63.

"divided duty" Duster, *Crusade for Justice*, 255.

"After being" Duster, *Crusade for Justice*, 16.

Chapter 8

"For it was the custom" Sinclair, *The Jungle*, 160.

"both sides" Engs, *Unseen Upton Sinclair*, 5.

"often caused" Engs, *Unseen Upton Sinclair*, 6.

"daily lesson" Sinclair, *Autobiography*, 7.

"When he was finally" Engs, *Unseen Upton Sinclair*, 7.

"went through" Engs, *Unseen Upton Sinclair*, 7.

"this new gold mine" Sinclair, *Autobiography*, 34.

"prematurely serious," Sinclair, *Autobiography*, 45.

"It will set forth," Sinclair, *Appeal to Reason*, 1.

"There were men" Sinclair, *The Jungle*, 116.

Chapter 9

"How lovely" Frank, *Tales from the Secret Annex*, 143.

*

BIBLIOGRAPHY

✻ *Titles suited to younger readers*

Abbott, John S.C., *Madame Roland, Makers of History*. New York: Harper & Brothers Publishers, 1904.

✻ Bausum, Ann. *Muckrakers: How Ida Tarbell, Upton Sinclair, and Lincoln Steffens Helped Expose Scandal, Inspire Reform, and Invent Investigative Journalism*. Washington, DC: National Geographic Society, 2007.

Bly, Nellie. *Among the Mad*, Godey's Lady's Book, Philadelphia: Louis A. Godey Publisher, 1889.

Brady, Kathleen. *Ida Tarbell: Portrait of a Muckraker*. Pittsburgh: University of Pittsburgh Press, 1989.

DeCosta-Willis, Miriam, ed. *The Memphis Diary of Ida B. Wells: An Intimate Portrait of the Activist as a Young Woman*. Boston: Beacon Press, 1995.

Douglas, George H. *The Golden Age of the Newspaper*. Westport, Connecticut: Greenwood Press, 1999.

Duster, Alfreda M., ed. *Crusade for Justice: The Autobiography of Ida B. Wells*. Chicago: The University of Chicago Press, 1970.

Engs, Ruth Clifford, ed. *Unseen Upton Sinclair*. Jefferson, North Carolina: McFarland & Company, 2009.

✻ Frank, Anne. *Tales from the Secret Annex*. New York: Bantam Books, 1994.

✻ Fritz, Tri. *The Nellie Bly Collection: The Books*. Bloomington, Indiana: Xlibris Corporation, 2012.

Goodman, Matthew. *Eighty Days: Nellie Bly and Elizabeth Bisland's History-Making Race Around the World*. New York: Ballantine Books, 2013.

Goodwin, Doris Kearns. *The Bully Pulpit— Theodore Roosevelt, William Howard Taft, and the Golden Age of Journalism*. New York: Simon & Schuster, 2013.

Hillstrom, Laurie C. *Defining Moments: The Muckrakers and the Progressive Era*. Detroit, Michigan: Omnigraphics, Inc., 2009.

Kroeger, Brooke. *Nellie Bly: Daredevil, Reporter, Feminist.* New York: Random House, 1994.

✳ Macy, Sue. *Bylines: A Photobiography of Nellie Bly.* Washington, DC: National Geographic Society, 2009.

Ockerbloom, Mary Mark, ed. *Nellie Bly's Book: Around the World in Seventy-Two Days.* University of Pennsylvania, Digital Library, 2000.

Pascal, Janet B. *Jacob Riis: Reporter and Reformer.* New York: Oxford University Press, 2005.

✳ Peck, Ira, ed. *Nellie Bly's Book Around the World in 72 Days.* Brookfield, Connecticut: Twenty-First Century Books, 1998.

Riis, Jacob A. *How the Other Half Lives: A Jacob Riis Classic.* Cedar Lake, Michigan: Reada-Classic, 2010.

———. *The Making of an American.* New York: The Macmillan Co., 1901.

Roosevelt, Theodore. "The Man with the Muck-rake." Speech text, Voices of Democracy, http://voicesofdemocracy.umd.edu /theodore-roosevelt-the-man-with-the-muck -rake-speech-text/. University of Maryland, 2006.

Royster, Jacqueline J., ed. *Southern Horrors and Other Writings: The Anti-Lynching Campaign of Ida B. Wells, 1892–1900.* Boston and New York: Bedford/St. Martins, 1997.

Schechter, Patricia A. *Ida B. Wells-Barnett & American Reform—1880–1930.* The University of North Carolina Press, 2001.

Sinclair, Upton. *Appeal to Reason.* Kansas: February 11, 1905.

———. *The Autobiography of Upton Sinclair.* New York: Harcourt, Brace & World, Inc., 1962.

———. *The Jungle.* New York: Doubleday, Page & Company, 1906.

Tarbell, Ida M. *All in the Day's Work: An Autobiography.* Urbana: University of Illinois Press, 2003.

Weinberg, Arthur, ed. and Lila Weinberg, ed. *The Muckrakers.* Urbana: University of Illinois Press, 2001.

INDEX

Photographs and drawings are indicated by italicized numbers.